Ann Snyder

A narrative of the civil war

For schools and colleges

Ann Snyder

A narrative of the civil war
For schools and colleges

ISBN/EAN: 9783337224639

Printed in Europe, USA, Canada, Australia, Japan

Cover: Foto ©ninafisch / pixelio.de

More available books at **www.hansebooks.com**

My country! 'tis of thee,
Sweet land of liberty,
  Of thee I sing:
Land where my fathers died!
Land of the Pilgrims' pride!
From every mountain side
  Let freedom ring!

A NARRATIVE OF THE CIVIL WAR.

BY MRS. ANN E. SNYDER
Nashville, Tenn.

FOR SCHOOLS AND COLLEGES.

NASHVILLE, TENN.:
PUBLISHING HOUSE METHODIST EPISCOPAL CHURCH, SOUTH
BARBEE & SMITH, AGENTS.
1899.

PREFACE.

This book is written in a plain, unvarnished style and chronologically arranged. It is a truthful narrative of the facts and events of the great War between the States, the civil war. It is intended to be a supplementary reader for schools, being an abridgment of the author's larger volume, "The Civil War." It was due the young that a suitable history of that struggle be placed in the schools, and the author was importuned to prepare it. The objection to most histories that have been written on the war is that they are of too large and bulky a character for the general reader. This history is written for the young, many of whom are teachers. It is the only one separate from United States History.

The introductory furnished by Capt. W. R. Garrett for this book is all-sufficient. He is one who served gallantly in the Army of Virginia.

With the earnest hope that this "NARRATIVE OF THE CIVIL WAR" may answer the purpose for which it was written it is sent forth into the hands of the public by

THE AUTHOR.

INTRODUCTORY.

The Sentiments of the Confederate Veterans.

The following extract from the report of the Committee on History of the United Confederate Veterans, made at the reunion at Richmond, Va., June 30, 1896, is given as an illustration of the patriotic sentiments felt by the surviving Confederate soldiers.

Reports were made by this committee at the Confederate reunions held at Birmingham in 1894, at Houston in 1895, at Nashville in 1897, and at Atlanta in 1898. They all use language sentiments similar to that quoted in the extract below. These several reports were unanimously adopted by the Confederate Veterans, and have been published as authoritative expressions of the surviving Confederate soldiers. They should be read by the boys and girls of the South, and will serve to inspire them with the noble and patriotic sentiments felt by the heroes who have proven themselves *great* in war and *magnanimous* in peace.

The Model and the Motto.

Participating in the enthusiastic sentiment which pervades the South, demanding that Southern pens shall vindicate Southern history, and recognizing the growing sentiment throughout the United States demanding a just and truthful record, your committee believe that they can see in the signs of the times a coming corps of vigorous Southern historians. We expect from them eloquence, candor, patriotism, philosophy, wisdom. Trusting into their hands the vindication of the South and of the Confederate soldier, we commend to them a model and a motto. The model is, "The Confederate soldier;" the motto is, "Let him live in history as he was in war and as he is in peace."

After the Confederate soldier had fought the war to the end, and had displayed fidelity, courage, and skill which have never been surpassed, he yielded when further resistance would have been folly and crime. When admiration for his valor and confidence in his honor led his antagonists to offer honorable terms, he accepted them in the same magnanimous spirit in which they were offered. He surrendered as the brave surrender. His surrender meant peace and conciliation. He obeyed the order to "ground arms." His tears and his musket fell together to the ground. The war was over. He had fought with honor, he surrendered with honor, and he has abided the issue with honor. He returned to the Union as an equal, and he has remained in the Union as a friend, with no humble apologies, no unmanly servility, no petty spirit, no sullen treachery. He is a cheerful, frank citizen of the United States, accepting the present, trusting the future, and proud of the past. He has built the New South— for there is a New South. But this New South is the legitimate offspring of the Old South. It is not a galvanized corpse worked into life by batteries without. It is a healthy expansion of forces from within. The New South is the work of the Confederate soldier, as the Old South was the work of his father. The Confederate soldier loves both. The New South, in material development, will rise above the Old South. We shall have a denser population, larger cities, more stately buildings, more ample revenues, more widely diffused intelligence, richer men, wealthier corporations; but we shall never have a higher social order, nobler sentiments, purer aspirations, grander men, or more devoted or truer women than the men and women of the Old South.

The Confederate soldier feels this, and he laments the Old South as a parent that has passed away. He turns to the New South as to his child, and with affectionate solicitude he devotes his life to rear and protect it. He knows the South is a part of the United States. He sees that its best interests demand peace and conciliation. In the language of the eloquent Georgian: "He is in the house of his fathers, and he has come to stay." He is a patriot by nature; he has never ceased to be a patriot.

THE STARS IN THE FLAG.

He must love some country, and he has no other country to love. He sees the stars and stripes float over the land. He gazes upon that flag, and counts its stars. Who placed them there? He traces the thirteen stars that represent the original States, and all the glorious history of the Revolution passes before his mind. He looks at the brilliant constellation that answers to the States formed from Western lands ceded by Virginia, the Carolinas, and Georgia. Who placed those stars in that firmament? His fathers. What venerated image comes before him when he gazes on that constellation which answers to the States formed out of the province of Louisiana? Thomas Jefferson. The stars that answer to the States formed from Florida and Oregon recall James Monroe. The lone star of Texas and the stars which glitter for golden California and the Mexican cessions bring up the memories

INTRODUCTORY.

of John Tyler and James K. Polk. While these shining witnesses bear their silent testimony, the territorial growth of the United States expands before his vision, and the Confederate soldier honors the flag which cannot wave without testifying to this great work of the South, while it proclaims alike the glory of the American Union. He learned to love that flag when he was a boy. He loved it even when he fought it. Every impulse of his generous nature prompts him to love "Dixie" and the "Star-Spangled Banner."

The Confederate soldier is a patriot of the highest type. He was a soldier because he was a patriot. He is a peaceful citizen because he is a patriot. He has forgiven the war, with its attendant injustice of invasion and reconstruction. He has risen above the humiliation of surrender. From the hero of war he has grown to be the hero of peace. In this character he deserves to be painted by history.

MODEL FOR THE HISTORIAN.

Then let the Confederate historian be like his model, the Confederate soldier. He must be patriotic, for he is representing the cause of patriots. He must be candid, for a partisan work will not live in history, and will fail to convince the world. He must be accurate, for even slight inaccuracies would be detected and would cast suspicion on his work. He must be patient in research, for much of his material is scattered and difficult of access, and he must make no assertion that is not sustained by evidence. He must be philosophical; calm and logical treatment is essential to the discussion of the social, economic, and political problems of the great confederated republic, the conflict of whose centrifugal and centripetal forces has baffled the philosophy of the Old World. He must be enthusiastic, but his enthusiasm must be restrained by judgment. This enthusiasm must be both sectional and national, and this judgment must be both minute and comprehensive. He must be bold and fearless, but always liberal. He must be eloquent, for he is dealing with a lofty theme, the most gigantic internal struggle which history records, the grandest contribution which the nineteenth century has made to human greatness, America's proudest title to martial glory. He is painting for future ages the picture of that eventful epoch whose memories are the joint heritage of all Americans, and which is destined to occupy in American history the pathetic place which the war of the roses now occupies in the annals of England and in the hearts of Englishmen.

In the foreground of this historic picture your committee would place a noble pile of Parian marble, pure and chaste, strong and enduring, on whose high summit there shall kneel the figure of the Southern woman, the guardian angel of the

Confederacy, with eyes turned to heaven, and sacred hands extended in unceasing blessings on the heads and hearts of the fathers, husbands, brothers, and sons of our Southland.

Respectfully submitted.

STEPHEN D. LEE, *Chairman;*   H. A. NEWMAN,
W. R. GARRETT,   W. P. CAMPBELL,
J. N. STUBBS,   F. S. FERGUSON,
CLEMENT A. EVANS,   WINFIELD PETERS,
ELLISON CAPERS,   J. O. CASLER,
S. G. FRENCH,   W. Q. LOWD.

ILLUSTRATIONS.

	PAGE
FORT SUMTER IN 1861	57
BATTLE BETWEEN THE MONITOR AND THE MERRIMAC	57
DESTRUCTION OF COTTON AT THE TAKING OF NEW ORLEANS	69
HARPER'S FERRY	69
DESTRUCTION OF THE HATTERAS BY THE CONFEDERATE STEAMER ALABAMA	85
THE SUMTER RUNNING THE BLOCKADE, AND CHASED BY THE FEDERAL SHIP IROQUOIS	85
COL. JOHN OVERTON'S RESIDENCE, GEN. HOOD'S HEADQUARTERS AT THE BATTLE OF NASHVILLE	187
MR. WILMER MCLEAN'S RESIDENCE, WHERE GEN. LEE SURRENDERED	187

MAPS.

BATTLEFIELD OF FORT DONELSON	32
NORTHERN VIRGINIA	93
BATTLEFIELD OF GETTYSBURG	98
NAVAL ENGAGEMENT IN MOBILE BAY	155
BATTLEFIELD OF FRANKLIN	166
BATTLEFIELD OF NASHVILLE	170
SHERMAN'S MARCH TO THE SEA	174

CONTENTS.

CHAPTER I.
The Causes 9

CHAPTER II.
The Secession of the States 13

CHAPTER III.
Affairs in Missouri 23

CHAPTER IV.
Battle of Cheat Mountain 26

CHAPTER V.
Fort Donelson—Permanent Organization 31

CHAPTER VI.
Affairs on the Water 38

CHAPTER VII.
Gens. Van Dorn and Sibley in the West 41

CHAPTER VIII.
Island No. Ten—Shiloh—New Orleans 43

CHAPTER IX.
Gallant Defense of Richmond 47

CHAPTER X.
A Series of Important Events 53

CHAPTER XI.
Movements in the West Again 64

CHAPTER XII.
Campaign in Northern Virginia 74

CONTENTS.

CHAPTER XIII.
MURFREESBORO—GALVESTON—ARKANSAS POST........... 79

CHAPTER XIV.
IMPRESSMENT—BATTERIES AND GUNBOATS............... 88

CHAPTER XV.
CHANCELLORSVILLE—VICKSBURG—GETTYSBURG 92

CHAPTER XVI.
SIEGE OF CHARLESTON—MORGAN'S RAID............... 104

CHAPTER XVII.
CHICKAMAUGA—MARTIAL LAW IN KENTUCKY............ 110

CHAPTER XVIII.
RAPPAHANNOCK—MISSIONARY RIDGE..................... 116

CHAPTER XIX.
MINOR OPERATIONS IN THE WEST....................... 124

CHAPTER XX.
INVASION OF MISSISSIPPI AND ALABAMA................. 131

CHAPTER XXI.
IN VIRGINIA AGAIN...................................... 137

CHAPTER XXII.
GEN. SHERMAN IN THE SOUTH........................... 146

CHAPTER XXIII.
BATTLE OF MOBILE BAY—GEN. GRANT IN VIRGINIA...... 154

CHAPTER XXIV.
BATTLE OF FRANKLIN, TENN............................ 165

CHAPTER XXV.
THE END.. 182

APPENDIX... 191

A NARRATIVE OF THE CIVIL WAR.

CHAPTER I.

THE CAUSES.

From the very character of the people that settled what is known as the Northern or, more strictly, the New England States, and those that settled in the Southern section of the country, one can easily see that in the course of the peculiar development of each natural and distinct lines of difference will be the result. Consequently in the narration of the momentous struggle of the eventful years from 1860 to 1865 it is eminently proper to briefly outline the causes that led up to it, going back to colonial days, to explain the heated antagonism that fell like the burst of a storm cloud upon the country.

The emigrants that settled the New England States were, for the most part, religious malcontents. The memory of Marston Moor and Cromwell was still fresh, and the royal head of Charles rolling from the block was not the act of a distant past, but was close enough in time to be a reality. The restoration came, and with it the Puritan, who thought he saw all the result of his hard-fought victories swept away. He was against the house of Stuart and all the nobles that took their stand by its fortunes. Consequently, after having emigrated from the mother country, these feelings became more intense in character. In their new home, the foundations of which were laid from the persecutions which produced the civil war in England, they began to construct a civilization peculiarly their own—a civilization which was a compound of persecution and bigotry. Forgetful of their own unhappy past, they soon possessed qualities which made England to them an unkind stepmother. The district that they had settled was barren and rocky, consequently agriculture was followed only as a matter of necessity. This encouraged the growth of cities and city life, which proved a great success as time passed on.

Turning now to those colonies of the South, history shows a civilization purely imitative in character, differing in every essential feature from that developed at the North. These emigrants were neither political nor religious refugees, but were rather acting under the impulse of a venturesome age that made them leave their island home and seek the El Dorado of the new world. Now were they all English. The Huguenots came over. Those who had followed the white plume of good Henry of Navarre united their race and lineage with the descendants of the victors of Cressy and Poitiers. Here was a commingling of royal blood. The soil of this new country was fair and fertile beyond description. Consequently the greatest inducements were held out to the agriculturist, and, as a natural result, city life was here discouraged and the growth of large plantations inevitable.

THE SLAVERY QUESTION.

Into both sections—thus begun, indeed, under the same circumstances, but differing widely as to the character of the people who settled them and the nature of the civilization that must necessarily follow —negro slavery was introduced. Those who were in the civil war had no part in its introduction, but their ancestors before them. Little was thought that one day a great excitement would be kindled, which would light the world with its glare.

The slave was no profit to his owner save in agricultural pursuits. Therefore in the New England States he was very soon found to be out of place and a loss to his owner. Their owners found no difficulty in disposing of them at a fair price to the planters of the Southern States. It was soon discovered by their former owners that slavery is a curse and slaveholding a crime.

From the nature of the two questions as already outlined, one may see that a cause, however slight, may beget an antagonism which will grow in intensity as the years go by; until, finally, to natural divisions and distinctions artificial ones will be added. Among the latter differences the question of slavery became the all-important one; and one, too, that at a very early date in the history of the country created more bitter and more intense opposition than one would expect from the nature of the question alone.

As far back as 1787 controversies arose in regard to the slavery question.

In 1820 the admission of the State of Missouri furnished a cause for a battle with the discordant elements, the result of which was the forming of Mason and Dixon's line, which produced only a temporary peace. The aged Thomas Jefferson wrote to a friend in regard to this measure: " It [the question of slavery] sleeps, but is not dead. A geographical line coinciding with a marked principle, moral and political, once conceived of men, will not be obliterated; every new irritation makes it deeper."

The agitation of the slavery question became intensified into a kind of religious fanaticism. Failing to agree, the war had to come.

STATE RIGHTS AND CENTRALIZATION.

When any community or association of men develop into certain principles and opinions that grow and increase in force and intensity to such an extent as to call into existence two distinct divisions completely discordant with each other, so that the peace and welfare of either one or the other is threatened, then naturally a question of permanent separation arises.

There arose two very widely different interpretations of the questions: Federal Constitution, its power, its limitation, technically called "State rights;" and "centralization."

In the beginning the original colonies formed a defensive and offensive alliance in the war against Great Britain. At the termination of the Revolutionary war the league was formed and ratified into the United States of America, with the individual liberties of each State guaranteed. Therefore it cannot develop any particular right in any one section to interfere with systems recognized as legal and legitimate at the time of the original union of the States. It is that which Rome exercised over her provinces gained by the might of the sword, which Bonaparte exhibited after victories in Germany and Italy, and which England showed in her dealings with the American colonies.

CHAPTER II.

THE SECESSION OF THE STATES.

ACTUAL withdrawal from the Union began December 20, 1861, by the Legislature of South Carolina passing the ordinance of secession. Six days later Maj. Anderson, with the United States troops, evacuated Fort Moultrie, in Charleston harbor. In January, 1861, Florida seceded; followed by Mississippi on the 9th of the same month, Alabama on the 11th, Georgia on the 20th, Louisiana on the 26th, and Texas on February 1. Thus, in less than three months all the cotton States had left the Union by a unanimous vote of the people, and secured all fortifications except the one in Charleston harbor. Just one month from the secession of South Carolina, Jefferson Davis, of Mississippi; Messrs. Kilpatrick and C. C. Clay, of Alabama; and Yulee and Mallory, of Florida, resigned their positions in Congress.

The State of Virginia was not quite ready to secede. Accordingly, February 4, 1861, the Legislature met and passed a resolution for a peaceful settlement of the difficulties. At first this line of procedure seemed to meet with a favorable response. Shortly afterwards the Legislature was again called together, and an election was held, showing that a majority were opposed to an unconditional secession of the State. Subsequently Tennessee and North Carolina decided to call a convention. The apparent reluctance of these States to rush at once into the matter seemed to encourage the government authorities, believing that some of the slaveholding States on the border would remain in the Union.

THE CONFEDERACY ESTABLISHED.

Meantime the six seceded States began to take steps toward establishing a provisional government by a convention of delegates from each assembled at Montgomery, Ala., February 4, 1861. After four days' deliberation this body adopted a Constitution for the Confederate States of America, which differed very little from the Constitution of the United States of America. Hon. Jefferson Davis was elected President, and Alexander Stephens, of Georgia, Vice President. This new government began to make preparations to make good its claims among the nations of the earth. It began with gaining possession of different United States forts and arsenals. Fort Moultrie and Castle Pinckney, at Charleston, were captured by State troops; Fort Pulaski, at Savannah; Mt. Vernon, Ala., was taken, with twenty thousand stands of arms; Fort Morgan, in Mobile Bay; Forts Jackson, Philip, and Pike, near New Orleans, together with the customhouse and mint; arsenals at both Baton Rouge and Little Rock, Ark.

Martin Crawford and John Forsyth, both of Georgia, were sent as commissioners to Mr. Seward, Secretary of State at Washington, in regard to Fort Sumter. The United States government at this time was preparing for a siege, the commissioners being ignorant of the fact. The fleet, with reënforcements, appeared off the harbor April 12, 1861, at the same time threatening the city of Charleston. Mr. Walker, Confederate Secretary of War, ordered Gen.

Beauregard to demand the immediate surrender of Fort Sumter. In reply to the Confederate general Maj. Anderson wrote as follows: "I have the honor to acknowledge the receipt of your communication demanding the surrender of Fort Sumter and its evacuation, and to say in reply thereto that it is a demand with which my sense of honor and my obligation to my government prevent my compliance." Gen. Beauregard had now no other course save to accept the gauntlet of war thrown down to him. So April 12 he sent word by his aid to Maj. Anderson that he would open fire with his batteries one hour from that time.

The First Gun.

The signal shell that opened in real earnest the great struggle between the States of our great republic of America went from Fort Johnson with its red glare across the sky of that momentous dawn, April 12. This was followed by the fire from Fort Moultrie, Cummings' Point, and the floating batteries. The Federals endured in silence until evening, when they opened terrific fire. The bombardment of the Confederates began to tell. The garrison was driven from the barbette guns, and the walls began to crumble away. The Federal fleet off the harbor remained passive. Why they took no part in the fight is explained by Capt. Cox: "As we neared the land, heavy guns were heard, and the smoke and shells from the batteries that had opened fire on Fort Sumter were visible. Immediately I stood out to inform Capt. Rowan of the Pawnee, but met him coming in. He hailed me and asked for a pilot, declaring his intention of standing into the harbor and sharing the fate of his comrades in the army. I went on board and informed him I would answer for it that the government did not expect any such gallant sacrifice, having settled upon the policy indicated in the instructions to myself and Capt. Mercer."

On the shore Confederate troops were in raptures over the prospect of victory.

April 13 every Confederate battery opened fire upon Fort Sumter. In the afternoon a shot from Fort Moultrie tore the flagstaff from the walls of Fort Sumter. Seeing the desperate condition of the garrison, Gen. Beauregard sent three of his aids with a message to Maj. Anderson to the effect that, as his flag was no longer flying and his quarters in flames, he desired to offer him any assistance he might need. In a short time the flag of truce was flung to the breeze. After two days' bombarding Fort Sumter surrendered. Certainly it was a day of great rejoicing in Charleston. As a testimonial to the gallantry of Maj. Anderson, Gen. Beauregard not only agreed that the garrison might take passage for New York at their own convenience, but also allowed them to salute their old flag with fifty guns.

Proclamation of War.

April 14, 1861, the great proclamation calling for troops was sent forth as follows: "Having thought fit to call forth, do hereby call forth the militia of the several States of the Union 75,000 strong, in order to suppress said combination, and to cause the laws to be duly executed and enforced."

Antagonism begets antagonism of like proportion and equal degree, so the Southern States, one after another, refused to furnish the government troops. Gov. McGoffin, of Kentucky, tried to be neutral; while Gov. Ellis, of North Carolina, replied that he could take no part in violating the laws of the land.

On April 17 Virginia adopted the ordinance of secession, followed by Arkansas, May 4; North Carolina, May 20; and Tennessee, June 8.

April 19 saw the first drop of fratricidal blood. The United States troops, in passing through Baltimore, were attacked by the citizens.

On the same day (April 19) President Lincoln issued his proclamation declaring all ports of the South in a state of blockade, and threatening that any interference upon the high seas would be considered nothing less than piracy. Letters of marque had already been issued by the Confederate government. Just at this time Gen. Lee resigned his position in the regular army. He was at once placed in command in Virginia. The Federals evacuated Harper's Ferry on the same day of President Lincoln's blockade proclamation.

On May 20 the seat of the Confederate government was removed to Richmond, Va.

The first invasion of Virginia was begun by the Federals occupying Alexandria May 4, the State troops falling back and taking position at Fairfax C. H., under command of Gen. Bonham, of South Carolina.

BATTLE OF BETHEL.

On June 20 Col. J. Bankhead Magruder, who was intrenched at Great Bethel Church, nine miles south of Hampton, was attacked by Gen. Pierce, with four thousand Federal soldiers. A battery of Richmond howitzers were the first to receive them. They retreated from their guns, and Capt. Bridges, of the First North Carolina Regiment, retook them. They advanced to the charge bravely. After considerable amount of skirmishing and artillery firing, the Federals were heavily reënforced under command of Gen. Winthrop, who had excited the admiration of the Confederates by his conspicuous gallantry.

The partial victory of the Confederates at Bethel was followed by a disaster at Rich Mountain. The main body of Federals was under Gen. McClellan, twenty thousand strong, advancing toward Beverly, with the main object to get in the rear of Gen. Garnett, who had been placed in command of Northern Virginia. Gen. Garnett had taken a strong position at Rich Mountain, his forces being arranged as follows: Col. Pegram, with one thousand six hundred men; Gen. Garnett, with three thousand infantry and six pieces of artillery, intrenched on Laurel Hill; and McClellan, with seven thousand troops. Gen. Rosecrans had started by a convenient route with three thousand troops to strike Gen. Garnett's rear. Gen. Garnett instructed Col. Pegram to defend his position at all hazards, which order he gallantly obeyed. The Federals moved in the midst of a pouring rain, through the tangled and pathless woods. They were disappointed when they failed to surprise the little band upon the mountain, but they continued to advance under a terrible artillery fire that seemed to tear the forest asunder. Assaulted by more than three times their number, both front and rear, the condition of the Confederates was hopeless. Col. Pegram saw that his only chance was to try to escape. Col, Tyler, with his command, succeeded in doing so; but Col. Pegram, hearing that Gen. Garnett had evacuated Laurel Hill, was compelled to surrender. At Carrack's Ford Col. Taliaferro, with the Twenty-Third Virginia, occupied the high banks upon the right of the ford, but, having exhausted every cartridge, ordered those brave boys who wore the gray to retreat. At the next ford Gen. Garnett fell while encouraging this brave little remnant, who had contested every inch of ground, with everything against them.

CONFEDERATES WIN AT MANASSAS.

Up to this time the battles had been comparatively skirmishes. The first real contest was soon to begin. The two armies of Virginia had maneuvered and watched each other warily, like two huge monsters preparing for mortal combat.

The Federals were under a commander of reputation, and one, too, in whom they had all confidence: Gen. McDowell. The Congress of the United States being in session, holiday was given to permit all to be present at the anticipated victory.

The brigades of Gens. Longstreet and Bonham confronted the Federals and consumed the 17th, 18th, and 19th of July in preliminary skirmishes along Bull Run and near the northwest junction of Manassas Gap.

Gen. Joseph E. Johnston was ordered at once to form a junction with Gen. Beauregard. He reached Manassas on the 20th, and united the Seventh and Eighth Georgia Regiments, and the Fourth Alabama, under Gen. Bee, to Jackson's Brigade. He then assumed entire command of the forces concentrated here, which numbered thirty thousand, divided into eight brigades.

Soon after sunrise the Federals opened fire with a heavy cannonading in front of Gen. Evans at the stone bridge. The infantry opposed each other for over an hour, during which time the main body of Federals were crossing the Bull Run on Gen. Evans' left; Gen. Evans, finding that they had succeeded in making a crossing, moved to his left and was attacked by a column sixteen thousand strong, much in excess of his own numbers; while Gen. Burnside appeared in front near Wheat's Louisiana Tigers. The Federals were further reënforced by the Second Rhode Island Regiment and a mounted battery, while Sloan's Fourth South Carolina Regiment came to the assistance of the Confederates. The determined and never-faltering valor of Wheat's Tigers soon caused the Federals to retreat. To relieve this point against the overwhelming numbers that were being massed against it, Gen. Bee came in with the Seventh and Eighth Georgia (Col. Bartow), the Fourth Alabama, Second Mississippi, and two companies of the Eleventh Mississippi, together with Imboden's Battery and two guns of Washington Artillery of Louisiana.

Thus reënforced, Gen. Evans moved across the plain and took up an advanced position, which he must hold against fifteen thousand Federals. A dreadful conflict of an hour's duration now ensued. In the meantime Gen. Sherman had crossed the Bull Run and was threatening the Confederate right. Victory now seemed inclined to the Federals. The Confederates began to waver somewhat, but were checked for a time by Gen. Bee, and he too, having suffered terribly, was just on the point of being overwhelmed by the mere mass and dead weight of the vastly superior numbers of the Federals, when Gen. Jackson arrived. With the inexpressible grief of his heroic heart depicted on his countenance, Bee approached him and said: "General, they are beating us back." "Sir," said Jackson, "we must give them the bayonet." With renewed zeal and vigor, Bee rallied his men with the inspiring words: "There is Jackson standing like a stone wall; let us determine to die here, and we shall conquer."

Now was the crisis of the battle. Orders had almost fatally miscarried, so that Gen. Beauregard had to change his plans, which required the greatest amount of maneuvering to retrieve the almost lost field.

By noon it seemed as if all the pomp and glory of war, together with all its horrors and terrors, had been turned loose in this valley, filled with smoke and reverberating and reëchoing with the awful roar of the artillery, above which could be heard the old Southern yell, which had sounded its glad notes of victory before, in the wars with the savages, at New Orleans with Jackson, and on the plains of Mexico with Taylor and Scott, and in the war with Spain the old familiar yell is heard.

The Confederates' left seemed to be overpowered. Gen. Johnston charged to the front with the Fourth Alabama. At two o'clock Gen. Beauregard issued orders for the whole line to recover the positions they had lost, which was done with a determination which meant victory, every regiment being in action:

Holmes' Regiment, and a battery of artillery; six guns under Capt. Lindsay Walker, two regiments from Bonham's Brigade, with Kemper's four six-pounders, and five guns of Washington Artillery from New Orleans.

The brave Gen. Bee fell mortally wounded at the head of his regiment; a few yards from him a shot pierced the heart of Col. Bartow, while he was grasping the flag of his regiment. Col. Fisher was also killed. It now became the Federals' time to retreat, and, after a terrible resistance, they were driven across the pike.

Gen. Kirby Smith, with Elzey's Brigade of the Army of the Shenandoah and Beckham's Battery, had reached Manassas. The Federals had rallied and turned again on the Confederate left. Gen. Johnson ordered Gen. Beauregard to throw forward his whole line. The Federals were again driven back into the fields. They then scattered in every direction toward Bull Run. Early and Cocke's Brigades, and Beckham's Battery, with Stuart's Cavalry, continued to play upon the wagon trains. The fields seemed covered with the retreating blue masses, and the victorious Confederates continued to pursue. The wounded were left uncared for, and the dead left unburied.

No accurate account is given of the Federal killed and wounded at the battle of Manassas, which must have been enormous—it is stated 4,500. Confederate loss, killed, 369; wounded, 1,483.

CHAPTER III.

AFFAIRS IN MISSOURI.

About this time interesting events were taking place in the West. The Confederates encamped on the outskirts of the city of St. Louis had been forced to surrender. Gen. Jackson issued a call for fifty thousand soldiers, and Gen. Price placed in command Gens. Parson, Hindman, M. L. Clark, and Jeff Thompson, these troops being quartered at Booneville. On June 20 the Federal troops under Gen. Lyons took up their line of march in that direction.

The barefooted soldiers under Gen. Marmaduke resisted manfully. Col. O'Kane surprised the Federals while they were asleep in a large barn.

A severe battle was fought at Oak Hill. The Federals had ten thousand men, and lost in killed and wounded and prisoners two thousand; the Confederates captured six pieces of artillery and seven hundred stands of arms. Gen. Lyons was commanding the Federal troops in person, while the Confederates were under Gens. Slack, McBride, Parson, and Rains on the left, with Herbert's Louisiana Regiment in the center. Though undrilled, they bore themselves with great gallantry against the Federals in command of Gen. Sigel.

After this battle the Confederates repaired to the frontiers of Arkansas, commanded by Gens. Slack and Parson. The character and equipment of these Missourians deserve a notice in our narrative. With old fieldpieces charged with pieces of iron, trace chains, and battered stone they replied to those splendidly equipped Federal soldiers. Their coolness and desperation in trying times was remarkable; their valor brought forth the following lines from the Federal general, Sigel: "Was the like ever seen? raw recruits standing like veterans, bidding defiance to every discharge of batteries." This great military scientist looked only to the outward and artificial side of the soldier; he forgot that the heart is the purpose that stirs to action; it was home and fireside that prompted those brave Missourians to action.

The Federal general, Lyons, was left dead on the field. Gen. Price had his body nicely put away and shipped to his wife.

Missouri now wheeled herself into line with the other Southern States, by the Legislature in session at Neosho passing the ordinance of secession.

The battle of Lexington, Mo., added another star to the Confederate crown of victory in the West. Here were captured three thousand prisoners, among whom were Cols. Mulligan, Peabody, White, Grover, and Van Horn, with eighteen commissioned officers, besides guns and ammunition. There were also taken seven hundred and fifty horses and a hundred and fifty thousand dollars' worth of commissary stores—just what the Confederates were in great need of. Commenting upon this victory, Gen. Price adds another laurel to the soldiers of Missouri: "This battle demonstrated clearly the fitness of citizen soldiery for the tedious operations of a siege."

September 1, at a place called Blue Hills, which gave the name to the battle, Gen. D. R. Atchison and Col. Sanders attacked the Federals with reckless valor and daring, and drove them ten miles. The Confederates took a number of tents and many camp supplies that the Federals had left in their flight. The Federals received such heavy reënforcements under Gen. Fremont that Gen. Price thought it best to fall back. The retreat was accomplished successfully, through the consummate skill of Gen. Jeff Thompson with his "swamp" brigade.

CHAPTER IV.

BATTLE OF CHEAT MOUNTAIN.

RETURNING now to the East, we find matters still very active near Cheat Mountain. At Seay Creek, in the Kanawha Valley, Gen. Wise caused a retreat of three regiments of boys that wore the blue, and was expecting to do a great work, when the disaster at Rich Mountain exposed the little army of boys who wore the gray.

Gen. Floyd, however, met the Federals at White Sulphur Springs, which caused them to retreat. He then strengthened his position on the Gauley.

Gen. Lee arrived at the scene of action with reënforcements early in August, but on account of some misunderstanding a retreat was ordered without firing a gun. Having failed to dislodge the Federals, he went to the Valley for the purpose of examining his position, then proceeded to Sewell, where he found Gen. Wise in front of twenty thousand Federals. Gen. Rosecrans, thinking the Confederates outnumbered him, retreated in the night, much to the surprise of Gen. Lee.

Gen. Lee now withdrew to Gauley, leaving Gen. T. J. Jackson behind with twenty-five hundred soldiers. Gen. Jackson was attacked by the Federals, but repulsed them, his pickets holding them in check for over an hour. Believing that Gen. Jackson had a large number of soldiers, they retreated.

The severity of the weather now put an end to the campaign in Western Virginia for a while.

Gen. Floyd was sent to Cotton Mills, where he was attacked by Gen. Rosecrans. He retreated, and was afterwards transferred to Tennessee and Kentucky.

The Federal general, Stone, began to cross the Upper Potomac October 20, at Harrison's Landing. Five companies of Massachusetts soldiers under Col. Devins succeeded in making a crossing. A few hours later Col. Baker took command of the whole, with orders from Gen. Stone to drive the Confederates from Leesburg, who, under command of Gen. Evans, of Georgia (one of the conspicuous and heroic actors of the bloody field of Manassas), consisted of four regiments—the Eighteenth Virginia, and the Thirteenth, Seventeenth, and Eighteenth Mississippi. Lieut. Col. Jenifer, with the Mississippians, held approaches toward Leesburg; while Col. Hunter engaged the boys in blue in the woods. The Federals being reënforced, Col. Burt, with the Eighteenth Mississippi, received a heavy fire. Col. Featherston, with his boys in gray, came into action in double-quick time. The battle now became general along the whole line. The Thirteenth Mississippi was held in reserve. For two long hours the boys who wore the gray fought with desperation against those that wore the blue, forcing them to retreat across the river, tumbling and rolling and scrambling down the steep bluffs, with the shrieks of the drowning added to other horrors of the battlefield.

CUMBERLAND GAP.

To protect the mountain passes of East Tennessee, Gen. Zollicoffer was sent September 14, with several thousand brave boys, to Cumberland Gap. He wrote an order to Gov. McGoffin, of Kentucky, stating that the safety of Tennessee demanded that the Confederate authorities occupy these mountain passes. He advanced toward Somerset, causing retreat of the German, Gen. Schoepff, who believed that Gen. Hardee was on his left flank.

In occupying these passes it was the purpose of the Federals to have means open of invading Southwest Virginia and get possession of the salt works of Western Virginia. In the meantime the authorities of Kentucky demanded strict neutrality, requesting Gen. Polk to evacuate Columbus. Gen. Polk replied that he would do so if the Federals would do likewise.

At Russellville, in November, resolutions were adopted asking permission to be taken in as one of the Confederate States, and by the middle of December it was accepted, and George W. Johnson was chosen for Governor.

Battle of Belmont.

While engaged in finishing fortifications at Columbus Gen. Polk was attacked, November 17, by a strong force from Cairo. Hearing from Gen. Grant on the river, and trying to land on Missouri shore, six miles above Belmont, the Federals made several vain attempts to gain a flank movement. Col. Tappan's forces, together with the assistance of the Thirteenth Arkansas and the Ninth Tennessee, commanded by Col. Russell, repulsed them on the right; and on the left their defeat was due to the deadly fire of Beltzhoover's Battery. Gen. Pillow gave orders to charge bayonets, which was executed along the whole line, and the Federals retreated toward the woods.

Here, however, they received a large reënforcement, and the boys who wore the gray were forced to retreat. It seemed now that these boys must yield the palm of victory, when, just at the proper time, Col. Walker, with the Second Tennessee, crossed the river to the support of Gen. Pillow, getting in the Federal rear. Fresh troops came, whom, with the Eleventh Louisiana Regiment, he placed under command of Col. Marks. The Federals now turned their attention to the boats which were used in transporting the Confederates across the river, and opened a heavy fire upon them. To oppose this movement, Capt. Smith's Battery was located on the opposite bank of the river. Gen. Cheatham was pressing the Federals on their flank, Cols. Marks and Russell in the rear, while Smith's Artillery was thundering in front of them. Gen. Polk had crossed the river and reached the Federal surgical headquarters, where they captured needed supplies. At this battle Gen. W. H. Jackson was promoted to the rank of colonel for gallantry in command of the Seventh Tennessee, Capt. Carnes taking Capt. Jackson's place.

The Confederates lost in killed and wounded 632, while the Federals lost fully three times that number. Thus the battle of Belmont is recorded as a victory to the Confederates.

DEATH OF GEN. ZOLLICOFFER.

Resuming the narrative of the exploits of Gen. Zollicoffer in Eastern Kentucky, we find that he had moved his forces to Mill Springs, on Fishing Creek, January 1, 1862. Here Gen. Crittenden assumed command. The army was in great distress on account of want of provisions for both man and beast. The severity of the winter made their situation wretched. Gen. Crittenden began to charge Gen. Thomas, with ten thousand men, at Beech Grove. On January 19 the battle began in real earnest, Gen. Zollicoffer leading the front. The Federals were driven back. Just as Gen. Zollicoffer mounted the crest of a hill he was shot by Federal Colonel Fry, and fell back in the midst of his dearest friends, Battle's noble regiment of Tennesseeans. Lieut. Evans Shields, of Gen. Zollicoffer's staff, fell mortally wounded, and died at Somerset, Ky. H. M. Doak, of Nashville, was the last one of his comrades to see the gallant soldier. Maj. Henry Fogg was also mortally wounded, and carried from the field by his comrades. Gen. Crittenden was forced to retreat to Monticello.

In the meantime Gen. Albert Sidney Johnston was placed in command of the Western Army, and his line embraced sixty miles below Louisville, on the railroad. The Federals advanced to Munfordville, part of their forces crossing Green River to Woodsonville, where they were attacked and defeated by Gen. Hindman, December 17, 1861, with a loss of fifty killed.

Gen. Johnston was forced to abandon his position at Bowling Green, on account of the immense numbers, under Gen. Buell, threatening to overpower his army, for it is estimated that the Federal troops in Kentucky consisted of one hundred thousand, mostly Western men, the bravest men that wore the blue, which was fairly proved in almost every battle in which they participated.

CHAPTER V.

FORT DONELSON—PERMANENT ORGANIZATION.

The distinguished Federal general, Grant, moved up the Cumberland River, and, after a gallant resistance, forced the brave defenders of Fort Henry to surrender. He then proceeded against Fort Donelson. Here Gen. Johnston, knowing whom he was fighting, sent the best divisions of his troops to meet them.

February 6, 1862, Gen. Bushrod Johnson assumed command of Fort Donelson. Fort Henry fell on the same day, and on the 9th of the same month Gen. Pillow succeeded Gen. Johnson. Day and night the work was pushed on the fortifications.

The line of intrenchments commenced on a ridge south of Dover; westwardly for two miles; deflected northward, at the point held by Porter's Battery; and thence northwest a half mile to Hickman Creek. Porter's, Graves's, and Capt. Frank Maney's batteries were fearfully exposed while in action. The morning of February 12 found Gen. Buckner in command of the right, and Gen. Pillow the left. Capt. Porter's Tennessee battery occupied the advance, sweeping the road that led to the main Fort Henry road, flanking the intrenchments both to the right and to the left, and in this exposed condition the Confederates suffered terribly.

The Federals completely encircled the Confederate works without much resistance. On the night of the 12th the scene is described as follows: The atmos-

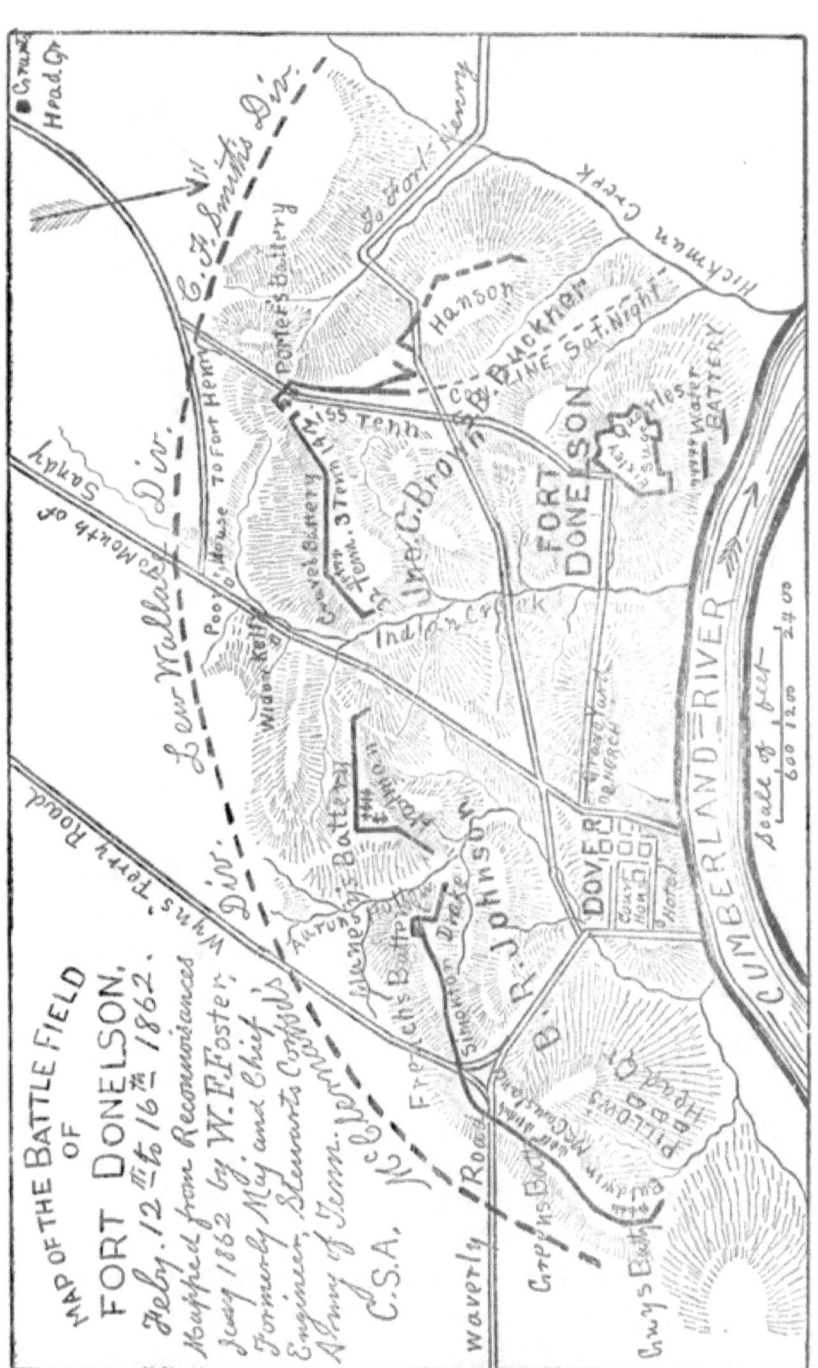

phere was springlike, the moon shone beautifully on those brave soldiers who were American citizens and wore the blue and gray; not a sound was heard save a stray shot from a picket who might be guarding the outpost. The dawn of the 13th was ushered in by the boom of artillery from the United States troops, which brought the boys in gray to their feet. Gen. Cook, with the Iowa men, sallied forth against the right center. Graves's and Porter's Batteries gave a warm reception to those Western men. The next attack was on the Confederates' left wing, by Gen. McClernand, which was responded to by Capt. Frank Green's Battery. For two hours the artillery fire was kept up all along the line. Also Capt. Maney's Battery, supported by Heiman's Brigade, engaged. At this point a heavy crossfire of artillery and small arms was forced upon the Federals. Gen. McClernand remarked: "The brave Illinoisans were truly badly worsted." Capt. Maney's men fought heroically. His lieutenant, Burns, was the first to suffer; his second lieutenant, Massie, was mortally wounded. For fifteen minutes these Western men stood their ground within fifty yards of the Confederate rifle pits; then they went down the hill; came up again and renewed their attack. This time the battery set fire to the leaves, and they went back the last time amid the cries of their comrades, wounded and dying and smothering from the smoke of the burning leaves and bushes. Col. John C. Brown discovered the approach of the Federals upon Gen. Heiman's center. He directed Capt. Graves to charge them, and within a short time the whole column was in full retreat. The brunt of this attack was borne by the Tenth, Fifty-Third, and Forty-Eighth Regiments of Tennessee, and Capt. Frank Maney's Battery. Col. Quarles's Forty-Second Tennessee arrived in time to share the glory, also to bear the losses. Gen. Smith's Federals made three distinct charges upon Gen. Hanson, but were forced to retreat. The gunboat Carondelet now opened upon the water batteries. Capt. Ross, with a sixty-four pound rifle, sent her disabled down the Cumberland. Capt. Dixon, a gallant young officer, was killed here. Capt. Tom Beaumont, of the Fiftieth Tennessee Regiment, was detailed, and rendered conspicuous service. Lieut. Hugh Bedford handled the one hundred and sixty-four pounder.

A fearful storm of snow and sleet now set in, which was almost unbearable.

On the morning of the 14th the lines were all readjusted. At three o'clock in the afternoon Admiral Foote steamed up with four ironclads and two gunboats, which bore upon the Confederate batteries. Capt. Jacob Culbertson, after the death of Capt. Dixon, commanded the water batteries. The furious cannonading from the fleet was harmless. The bolts of the Confederate guns went crashing through the iron and heavy timbers. Commodore Foote says: " I have commanded the taking of forts and in several naval engagements, but never under so heavy a fire as this before." It is said of him: " He wept like a child when the order to withdraw was given." The Confederate batteries were very little injured. As the great monsters retreated down the stream cheers and shouts filled the air, which seemed almost an inspiration.

1862. FORT DONELSON—PERMANENT ORGANIZATION.

Heavy reënforcements having arrived, a council of war decided to open a way to Nashville. Gen. Johnston telegraphed to "get the troops to Nashville if the forts could not be held." Gen. Floyd called a council of his general officers, when it was decided to attack the Federals' right at daylight. Gen. Pillow was to force the attack on the extreme left with Col. Baldwin's Brigade, Gen. Bushrod Johnson's Division; he to move out of the trenches, and Gen. Heiman to occupy the ditches; Head's Thirteenth Tennessee was to aid Gen. Pillow.

Next morning Baldwin moved, supported by Col. Forrest, on the left, upon Gen. McClernand's right, which was in battle line awaiting. McCausland, Simonton, and Wharton were engaged by McAuther and Lew Wallace, sustained by Schwartz's, McAllister's, and Dresser's Batteries. Instances of heroic courage were exhibited by both the blue and the gray. Many memorable individual hardships were endured by these brave ones.

Gen. Forrest caused Gen. Lew Wallace to abandon six pieces of artillery. Graves's and Porter's Batteries, on Wynn's Ferry Road, engaged in an artillery attack, aided by Gen. Bushrod Johnson's advance. Col. John C. Brown led his Tennesseans in person upon Aurora Hollow, the valley to the left of Gen. Heiman. Maney's, Graves's, and Porter's Batteries made bold charges. Capt. Porter was disabled, and while being borne from the field he spoke to his brave young lieutenant, John Morton, "Don't let them have my guns, Morton;" to which he replied, "Not while I have one man left." Gen. Forrest took up his line of march to Nashville, as did also

Gen. Pillow. Col. Johnson, finding no sentinels, pushed his way through.

After nine hours' struggle these soldiers could do no more, with only thirteen thousand effective soldiers, weakened by exposure and worn out by hard fighting. Great physical endurance and heroic courage was exhibited by both sides, being nearly all American citizens. Very few foreigners were engaged in this battle.

The Federal loss in killed and wounded and prisoners was fifteen thousand; Confederates' loss, five thousand.

The Confederates Evacuate Nashville.

On receiving news of the fall of Fort Donelson Gen. Johnson saw that Nashville could not be defended without causing the city to be bombarded, so determined upon its evacuation. When it was so determined, a wild panic extended to every point for miles in the country; none were expecting that to take place. Gov. Harris, with the Legislature, removed to Memphis. A large quantity of stores and provisions was lost. Even large numbers of sick and wounded soldiers had to be left in the hospital, but these were tenderly cared for by the citizens. Particularly did the ladies bestow great kindness.

Gen. Johnston meantime had reached Murfreesboro, and was resting the main body of his army there.

A Permanent Organization

was effected by the Confederate government on the 22d of February, 1862, when affairs did not look so bright for the young government as in the beginning.

It seemed almost impossible to furnish adequate protection at all points both on land and sea, but the best possible means were being taken. But the financial aspect of the war was encouraging; for there was no floating debt, the credit of the government was unimpaired with the people, and the total expenditures of the government for the year were one hundred and seventy million dollars. Moreover the recent reverses had a tendency to quicken the energies of the authorities, so as to produce vigorous and active measures, among which was the conscript bill.

All backsets had a tendency to intensify the devotion of the Southern people.

CHAPTER VI.

AFFAIRS ON THE WATER.

After the abandonment of Columbus by the Confederates, the defense of Island Number Ten, situated in a bend in the Mississippi river, near the towns of New Madrid and Point Pleasant, Mo., was intrusted to Gen. Beauregard. It was considered thoroughly impregnable.

On the 12th of October the submerged ram, the Manassas, made an attack upon the Federal squadron near the mouth of the Mississippi river, sinking the gunboat Preble, and driving the others from the river into the gulf.

A Confederate Naval Victory at Hampton Roads.

The Confederate squadron in the James river was commanded by Franklin Buchanan. The fleet consisted of the Virginia, which was the remodeled Merrimac, that had been partially destroyed; the steamer Patrick Henry, twelve guns; the steamer Jamestown, two guns; and the gunboats Teazer, Beaufort, and Raleigh. With these he moved out to Newport News, to offer battle to the Federals.

The Federal ship Congress, with a broadside, occupied a position below the batteries at Newport News, while the Cumberland was just opposite them. With a determination to sink the Cumberland with the Virginia, Capt. Buchanan steamed straight toward her, complimenting the Congress again with a broadside. The shore batteries, with both ships, now concentrated fire upon the Virginia, which kept straight on, raking the Cumberland fore and aft with the discharge of her guns, and striking her bow below the water with such terrible effect that in fifteen minutes the waters of the ocean rolled over the flag of the Cumberland. The Virginia was not satisfied with this success, but went to serve the Congress similarly. On account of the shallowness of the water, she could make but slow progress. She managed, however, to get in position above the James river batteries, though she had to endure a second time the Federal fire. They were thinking that the Confederate " terror " had sustained great injuries, so as to force her to withdraw from the contest; but when she turned a terrible broadside upon the Congress, producing death and destruction, dismay and confusion, a flag of truce was run up at the masthead, and the commander of the Beaufort was ordered to go and take possession of her, with officers as prisoners, but to allow the crew to land. He also ordered the ship burned.

An attempt was now made to burn the Congress, which the shore batteries prevented. At this failure Capt. Buchanan opened upon her with hot shots, and at midnight the citizens of Norfolk were awakened by the explosion of her magazine, and all that was left of the Congress was the scattered fragments floating upon the sea.

Capt. Buchanan having been seriously wounded, Lieut. Catesby Jones assumed command, and the Virginia sailed out to meet the ironclad, the Monitor. For two hours these vessels poured a terrible fire into each other. Once the Virginia ran aground, being under double fire of both the Monitor and the Minnesota. After having disabled both, the Virginia put back to Norfolk.

These exploits of the Virginia created great excitement both at the North and in Europe, and within five days after the defeat at Hampton Roads the Federal government appropriated fifteen million dollars for building ironclad vessels.

CHAPTER VII.

GENS. VAN DORN AND SIBLEY IN THE WEST.

In the latter part of January, 1862, the Federals were massing large numbers—first at Rolla and afterwards at Lebanon. Gens. Price and Van Dorn saw that they were getting a larger force than they could meet, and, as they expected, the Federals attacked them and forced a retreat from Springfield. The retreat was a bad one, as the Confederates had to fight their way through.

Gen. Van Dorn was appointed by President Davis to take command of the forces in the West, and on March 3d took charge of the united forces of Gens. Price and McCullough.

BATTLE OF ELK HORN.

At Sugar Creek twenty thousand Federals, under Gens. Sigel and Curtis, were waiting for reënforcements. On March 4 Gen. Van Dorn marched toward Sugar Creek, for the purpose of attacking the Federals.

On the morning of the 7th the battle began, and the Confederates were on the point of victory, when Gens. McIntosh and McCullough were both killed. Notwithstanding the loss of their commanders, those brave boys gained possession of the intrenchments. On the morning of the 8th the contest was renewed, and Gen. Van Dorn continued the desperate fight until after nine o'clock, when he withdrew in the direction of his supplies.

The Confederates lost in killed and wounded six hundred, while the Federal loss is considered twice that much, though it is not officially stated.

In the Far West.

After a long March of nearly two hundred miles from Arizona, Gen. Sibley, with two thousand three hundred troops, found himself near Fort Craig, in which were United States troops to the number of six thousand, one thousand five hundred of whom were American soldiers, and about five thousand Mexicans. Having crossed the Rio Grande river, Col. Pryor came in contact with the Federals. With a second attack the Confederates were forced to retreat and take up a new position. Thinking that they had won a great victory, the Federals moved their batteries across the river, which was no sooner done than the Confederates charged them, and, with the assistance of Teel's Battery, drove them from their guns and forced them to recross the river.

In this battle of Valverde, March 21, the Confederates lost 38 killed and 120 wounded, while the Federals lost in killed, 300, 400 wounded, and 2,000 Mexicans missing. The Confederates continued their march, forcing the Federals to evacuate both Albuquerque and Santa Fé.

CHAPTER VIII.

ISLAND NO. TEN—SHILOH—NEW ORLEANS.

MARCH 15 Flag Officer Foote began the bombardment of Island No. Ten, which had been so finely fortified by Gen. Beauregard. Gen. Beauregard left to take charge of operations on the Tennessee river. Gen. McCown was ordered to take charge of the island. On his arrival he found the Federals had succeeded in cutting a canal across the bend of the river, on the Missouri side, three miles above the island, to Bayou St. John. Gen. McCown built flatboats, and thereby secured his retreat.

On April 1 Gen. McCown was relieved of his command. April 6 Gen. McCall moved the infantry to the Tennessee shore. The Federal gunboats having passed the island in a fog, it now became a necessity to surrender this "Gibraltar of the Mississippi."

THE GREAT BATTLE OF SHILOH.

In massing all his forces at Corinth Gen. Beauregard's purpose was to cut off the Federals' communication between the South and East. Gen. Johnston moved from Murfreesboro and took command; also two divisions of Gen. Polk's forces at Columbus, together with several Louisiana regiments, and troops from Mobile.

Gen. Grant occupied a position at Pittsburg Landing, awaiting the arrival of Gen. Buell, who was hastening from Nashville to join him. To prevent a junction with Gen. Grant was the object of Gen.

Johnston. After much skirmishing the great battle of Shiloh was opened April 6 by Gen. Hardee advancing against the camp of the Federals while they were at breakfast, taking them by surprise, and finding them unprepared. However, they quickly formed to meet the boys in gray, who were advancing in three lines, with Gen. Hardee commanding the front, Gen. Bragg the center, and Gen. Polk the rear. A sublime artillery duel began this work of death, and the splendid composure of these soldiers of our country who wore the blue and gray under this test gave prophecy of the magnificent courage which each side displayed on that memorable day. Rising from the ground, on which they were lying that the artillery fire might pass over them, they rushed forward, crushing everything before them. The scenery is described as follows: Far up in the air shells burst forth like shattered stars, and passed on in little clouds of white vapor; while others filled the air with a shrill scream and burst far in the rear. All along the line the faint smoke of musketry rose lightly, while from the mouth of the cannon intense white smoke burst up all around.

At half past two Gen. Johnston, commander in chief of the Confederate forces, fell mortally wounded. Riding up to him, Gov. Harris asked him if he was badly hurt. The dying hero replied: "Yes; I fear mortally." He fell from his horse, and soon passed away. The Confederates soon continued to push the Federals to the Tennessee river. On Sunday night Gen. Beauregard established his headquarters at the little church at Shiloh. The soldiers of both armies slept on their arms. Gen. Grant was relieved by the glistening bayonets of Gen. Buell's command. Gen. Buell was hailed to the field of slaughter with cheers. To avert further sacrifice of human life Gen. Beauregard agreed to withdraw his forces, being unable to stand longer such overpowering numbers. Approaching Gen. Breckinridge, he said: "Gen. Breckinridge, it may be you will sacrifice your life; this retreat must not be a rout; you must hold the Federals if it takes your last man." "Your orders shall be executed," replied Gen. Breckinridge.

The Federals lost nearly all their artillery, over three thousand prisoners, a division commander, several brigade commanders, an immense supply of subsistence and ammunition, and a large number of means of transportation.

On Sunday the Confederates were engaged with the commands of Gens. Prentiss, Sherman, Hurlburt, Smith, and McClernand. The Confederates suffered much from loss of officers. Gen. Gladden, of South Carolina, fell mortally wounded; also Gov. George W. Johnson, of Kentucky; Gen. Bray had two horses shot from under him; Gen. Breckinridge was struck twice; Maj. Gen. Hardee had his coat torn by minie balls; Gen. Cheatham received one in the shoulder; Gen. Bushrod Johnson was wounded in the side; Col. Adams, of Louisiana, Colkit Williams, of Memphis, and Gen. William B. Bate, of Tennessee, received several injuries; and Col. Blythe, of Mississippi, was among the killed.

The Confederate loss in this terrible battle was 10,000, while the Federal loss was 20,000.

Gen. Beauregard retired to Corinth as a strategic point.

Fall of New Orleans.

New Orleans was considered impregnable. The city was occupied by a large force under Gen. Lovell, and in its harbor was a fleet consisting of twelve gunboats, one ironclad steamer, and the famous ram, Manassas. The Federal fleet engaged was forty-six sail, carrying two hundred and eighty-six guns and twenty mortars, the whole under the command of Admiral Farragut, a distinguished officer. April 24 the Federal fleet opened fire on the Confederate fleet, which was vigorously returned. In one hour several Federal boats succeeded in passing the forts, the first one in disguise, having Confederate night signals flying, which allowed her to pass the Confederates unmolested. On receiving this news the whole city was thrown into intense excitement. The conflict between the fleets was of a dreadful character. The Confederates burned their vessels, and drove them to shore. The Manassas was sunk, and the great ironclad Louisiana was not in good working order. Gen. Lovell withdrew his army to save the city from destruction. The evacuation was begun April 24. As soon as the Federal fleet came along the river the work of destruction began. For five miles along the river the cotton was piled and burned, preventing its being confiscated by the Federals. Great steamers wrapped in flames floated down the river. Fifteen thousand bales of cotton were consumed. The city was left in charge of Mayor Monroe, Gen. Butler taking possession May 1.

CHAPTER IX.

GALLANT DEFENSE OF RICHMOND.

TURNING now for a brief glance at civil affairs, the government at Washington, astonished at the prolongation of the war, was worried at the failure of Gen. McClellan to take Richmond. Consequently the Secretary of War issued instructions to the commanding generals to seize upon any and all private property.

At the South the government began to despair of foreign recognition. The disaster at New Orleans put an end to all their hopes in this respect. To increase the number of soldiers it became necessary to pass a conscript bill, which was done in May, 1862. This created a considerable opposition in the minds of the people, inasmuch as they considered it a reflection upon them.

KERNSTOWN—JACKSON REPULSED.

March 23 we find Gen. Jackson attacking the Federals at Kernstown, near Winchester, Va., with six thousand troops, among which was Capt. McLaughlin's Battery and Col. Ashby's Cavalry. The battle continued until dark, when Gen. Jackson fell back to Cedar Creek, having sustained a loss of one hundred in killed and wounded.

With the Federal forces enveloping Richmond, both from the land and from the river, one can see the necessity for vigorous action. The repulse of the Federal gunboats upon their attack on the batteries at Drewry's Bluff, under command of Capt. Farrand, May 13, caused them to retreat.

Battle of Williamsburg.

May 5 Gen. Hooker's Division came near Williamsburg, with the rear guard commanded by Gen. Longstreet, the Federals being in a forest near Williamsburg. Gen. Hooker came out of the forest, was attacked and forced back. Gen. Shields came to his assistance. Gen. Longstreet engaged nine brigades under Gen. McClellan from sunrise until sunset, thereby securing Gen. Johnston's safe retreat. He had won a brilliant victory. Gen. McClellan agreed to a loss of 450 killed and 1,400 wounded. Gen. Longstreet carried with him heavy artillery, the design being that Gen. Franklin should move to West Point, at the head of York River, and land forces there to attack Gen. Johnson. May 7 Gen. Franklin tried to land under protection of gunboats, at Barhamsville, but was forced to retreat by Whiting's Division of Texas troops. Franklin hurried back to his flotilla. He was compelled to abandon Yorktown.

Jackson's Successes in the Valley.

Gen. Jackson was sent into the Valley of Virginia, the object being the concentration of forces, which took place immediately around the city of Richmond. May 8 Gen. Jackson proceeded to attack Gen. Milroy, with twelve thousand troops, at McDowell. Gen. Jackson being thrice outnumbered by the Federals, the irresistible charge of Johnston's Brigade (consisting of Virginia Volunteers and the Twelfth Georgia Regiment), just as the sun was going down after a beautiful day, caused the Federals to retreat. This was a costly victory to Gen. Jackson, in that he lost three hundred and fifty killed and wounded; Federals, seven hundred.

Gen. Jackson moved upon Gen. Banks at Port Royal, seizing a lot of artillery and fourteen hundred prisoners. Gen. Banks, thoroughly alarmed, retreated toward Winchester. May 24 Gen. Jackson struck Gen. Banks's retreating column. The Federals managed to reach Winchester, however, only to be again met on the 25th by Gen. Jackson. Of these proceedings we quote from the Federal commander, who has proved himself to be a great man, "Pursuit by the enemy was prompt and vigorous, but our movements were rapid," which fact the general truthfully relates of those boys who wore the gray. The Confederates lost only a few men, but they captured four thousand prisoners, and much supplies for man and beast.

GEN. JACKSON DEFEATS THE FEDERALS AT PORT REPUBLIC.

Gen. Jackson fell back from Winchester between the two forces of Fremont and Shields, the former numbering twenty thousand and the latter ten thousand. He then marched toward Port Republic, and was attacked by the Federal General, Fremont, on June 8, while Shields's Division was coming upon the other bank (east) of the Shenandoah river. Thus, so to speak, between two fires, he left that portion of his troops under Gen. Ewell to look after Gen. Fremont, while he kept Gen. Shields on the other side of the river, displaying a remarkably good judgment in the management of the fight. When night came, it was found that Gen. Ewell had driven the Federals back, with two thousand killed and wounded, while his own loss was less than two hundred. Under cover of darkness Gen. Jackson moved across North River, leaving a few boys behind to keep the distinguished man, Gen. Fremont, from following him. So on Monday he began to attack the Federals, who were waiting patiently on the east bank of the Shenandoah. At first Gen. Jackson had his hands full. So well directed was the fire of the boys in blue that it did seem that our boys who wore the gray, who had stood so many battles, must give way. Fresh troops from Port Republic were rapidly coming to their assistance. Gen. Taylor, with the Louisiana regiment, came out of the woods and charged up to the mouths of the cannon. The whole Federal line now gave way, the Confederates pursuing for twelve miles, taking five hundred prisoners. Jackson retired to Brown's Gap.

Battle of Seven Pines.

May 30 Gen. Johnston found the enemy in front of him on the Chickahominy river, so he determined to attack them the next day at dawn. For some reason Gen. Longstreet failed to get expected support, and the battle was opened without assistance. Gen. D. H. Hill's brave boys, who were proud to wear the gray, charged grandly, penetrating the Federal intrenchments. It was found that the Federals held their position a while during the night, and darkness only prevented another defeat. The brave Tennessee-an, Gen. Robert Hatton, was killed. The Confederate loss was four thousand; the Federal loss, eight thousand men, ten pieces artillery, and six thousand muskets. Gen. Johnston having been wounded, the command of the Confederate forces at Richmond devolved upon Gen. Robert E. Lee.

Mechanicsville—Malvern Hill.

The Federal lines along the Chickahominy extended twenty miles on both sides of the stream, with a purpose of threating Richmond with a siege. That series of splendid battles along this celebrated little stream was begun by Gen. Jackson June 26. A portion of the Federals left the north bank near the Brooke Turnpike.

Gen. A. P. Hill had crossed the river at Meadow Bridge; and at Mechanicsville, without waiting for orders to join Gen. Jackson, he hurled his column of fourteen thousand against the Federals, who resisted bravely, but finally they retreated to Powhite Swamp.

On Friday, with Gen. A. P. Hill in the center, and Gens. Longstreet and D. H. Hill coming from the Chickahominy, Gen. Jackson toward the left at some distance charged the Federals, and by eight o'clock in the evening the Federals had retreated from the north to the south side of the Chickahominy. It is right to mention in our narrative the brilliant military action of Gen. A. P. Hill upon the forces stationed at Gaines's Mills. Gen. Hill was supported by Gen. Pickett's Brigade, from Gen. Longstreet's Division. Whiting's Division of Texans must here come in for a record of superior valor and making a masterly double-quick charge.

Having been forced to leave all their strongholds on the north bank, with communication cut off from Washington, the Chickahominy barring their way in front, Gens. Longstreet, Magruder, and Huger pressed close to their rear, Sunday morning it was discovered that they had left their fortifications, and had massed their forces five miles northeast of Darbytown, at a place known as Frazier's Farm. Finally Gens. Longstreet and Hill moved forward unsupported, while the Federals received them with a terrible fire from infantry and artillery.

The Confederates, with as brilliant courage as ever illustrated the annals of war, moved on in the midst of shot and shell, the Federals gradually falling back. From their hard struggle of the day the whole armies were worn out, consequently they retreated before fresh troops. At eleven o'clock Gen. Magruder arrived and intrenched on Carter's Farm. In this battle, known as Malvern Hill, was the last important incident of the drama of Richmond, a great catastrophe for Gen. McClellan: Federal forces, 105,825; Confederates, 62,695; Confederate losses during command of Gen. Johnston, 6,084. Gen. Lee, in taking command, had only 56,612; reënforcement, 24,150; total, 80,762. Confederate losses under Lee and Johnston, 19,000. McClellan reached the James river with 85,000 to 90,000 men, pursued by Gen. Lee with 60,000.

CHAPTER X.

A SERIES OF IMPORTANT EVENTS.

Just when the great armies in Northern Virginia were marshaling their forces for the great conflict on the Chickahominy, farther South an inspiring victory was gained by those who wore the gray. At Secessionville, on James Island, near Charleston, S. C., a large force of United States troops made an attack on the intrenchments of Col. J. G. Lamar. Three times they made brave charges, but retreated, leaving four hundred prisoners.

After Shiloh, Gen. Beauregard had intrenched himself at Corinth, Miss., and made an effort to get the Federals to attack him. Failing in this, he moved his camping ground June 7 to Tupelo, a better position. The Federal troops occupied possession of Memphis, Tenn., June 6. They then turned their attention to Vicksburg, Miss., but here they met an unexpected disappointment. After a siege of six weeks, during which time they threw twenty-five thousand shells into the city, they abandoned the fruitless effort.

Between the 4th and 28th of July Gen. John H. Morgan effected his famous raid. He started from Knoxville, Tenn., with rangers from Georgia, Texas, and Tennessee, and pushed his way through a country where were to be found many who did not agree with his brother of the South. He captured a large number of prisoners, with three thousand stands of arms, at Lebanon, Ky.

Content with this brief summary of military operations in the West, we now turn our narrative to the ever-interesting scenes in Virginia. Every foot of its historic ground is a battlefield, through which the military student of all after times (those whose wore the blue and the gray) may find illustrated the highest ideals of his art and the loftiest examples of soldierly courage and endurance. On July 23 Gen. Pope was transferred from the West to the Army of Northern Virginia. He now took up his line of march toward the interior of Virginia, penetrating as far as ten miles east of Culpepper Courthouse. Against this movement Gen. Jackson was sent. On hearing that the latter had crossed the Rapidan, Gen. Pope sent Gen. Banks to stop him.

August 12 Gen. Ewell's Division moved forward and took position at Cedar Mountain, and opened artillery fire on the Federals. The battle began in real earnest by the attack of Gen. Early's Brigade upon the Federals. The brave Gen. Winder perished as he was leading Gen. Jackson's Division. The Federals made a desperate charge through an open cornfield with cavalry, which created a temporary confusion, but the Confederates soon recovered themselves and made a desperate charge, when night began to throw its black mantle over a scene fraught with horrors. The Federals retreated to the woods, leaving on the fields of Cedar Mountain nearly two thousand dead, five hundred prisoners, one thousand stands of arms, one dozen wagon loads of ammunition, two Napoleon guns, and a large amount of new clothing.

The Federal government now determined to unite

the two large armies of Pope and McClellan. Gen. Lee, learning that fact, rapidly made change in his position of forces, and on August 17 held them in front of Gen. Pope to prevent his crossing the Rapidan.

By a rapid march of two days over the mountains, the great Jackson, misleading the Federals, succeeded in occupying Bristow and Manassas Stations on August 27, capturing thousands of dollars' worth of supplies. On the same day the Federals made an attack on both positions. Gen. Taylor's Brigade of Slocum's Division of the Army of the Potomac attacked Manassas, but retreated toward Centerville. Gen. Hooker's Division moved against Gen. Ewell at Bristow, forcing him back across the Muddy Run. Gen. Jackson, by a masterly movement, succeeded in getting an advantageous position on the old battlefield of Manassas, so inspiring from its memories of that former greatness which seemed soon to be repeated. Gen. Stewart caused a retreat of the Federal cavalry near Gainesville, on the Warrenton Pike, and later in the day Gen. Jackson threw his forces in front of the Federals, who were advancing to attack him near the village of Groveton.

Gen. Longstreet, in order to join his division with Jackson's, had to force his passage through a wild woods, a precipitous mountain pass known as Thoroughfare Gap. It was held by a force of two thousand Federals. With its rough and steep sides and narrow passways this gap would seem impossible to climb. The Confederates made the effort, and forced their way, with several badly hurt. The Federals as well as Confederates had to climb their way down the mountain. The Federals advanced with artillery. They were received by Gen. Ewell's Division, who reserved their fire until the Federals were close upon them, when they opened fire with terrible effect, which caused a retreat. Gen. Jackson, reënforced by Gen. Hood's Division, fought with renewed energy and caused the Federals to retreat. The Federal loss in killed and wounded was eight thousand. These attacks by the Federals were upon the wings of the Confederates.

August 30 saw Gen. Pope gathering his energies for another attack upon these poor, worn-out soldiers of Gen. Jackson, the latter being reënforced by Longstreet's Corps, which took the right, Jackson himself holding the left wing, the whole line forming a crescent five miles long. Opposed to these on the Federal side were Gens. Sigel, Fitz Porter, and Reno, in the center, and Heintzleman and McDowell on the left and right respectively. The Confederate batteries in the center, under Gen. S. D. Lee, opened rapidly. The Federals moved forward in three lines against Gen. Jackson's infantry. Desperately did these old veterans who wore the blue maintain themselves against those who wore the gray. They sacrificed all to redeem their trust to their brave commanders. To no purpose did this elect corps sacrifice their best blood in their efforts to save their country. Col. Stephen D. Lee turned batteries upon them, with Jackson and Longstreet watching the retreat. Gen. Sickles' Excelsior Brigade, famous for deeds of daring, met with a great drawback from Gen. Hood's Division. An order was now given for a general charge along the whole Confederate

Fort Sumter in 1861. (See page 15.)

Battle between the Monitor and the Merrimac. (See page 39.)

line. Gradually these gray masses moved forward, cheering as they went, and sounding their clarion peals of victory above the din of artillery and the rattle of musketry. Gen. Franklin met the retreating Federals with thirty thousand reënforcements. With these Gen. Pope restored partial order to his disorganized army, continuing his retreat to Washington City, leaving upon the battlefield a large amount of ammunition. Thirty-eight thousand Federals were killed and wounded; the Confederate loss was about one-half that number.

On September 4 Gen. Lee—leaving to his right Arlington Heights, to which Gen. Pope had retreated—crossed the Potomac into Maryland, his main object being to seize Harper's Ferry, and to test the people of Maryland. He then threw Pennsylvania into a state of consternation from Hagerstown. With the presence of the Confederate army at Frederick, and fearing an invasion of their territory, the North was filled with anxiety and terror. To carry on certain important movements, Gen. Lee had to divide his forces into three corps, commanded by Gens. Jackson, Longstreet, and Hill. He ordered Gen. Jackson to recross the Potomac at Williamsport and to get behind Harper's Ferry, with the purpose of preventing its capture. Gen. McClellan resumed command of the Federals September 14, Gen. Pope having lost his command.

The Battle of Boonsboro.

Gen. Jackson had separated his own division from the main body of the army in order to make his attack upon Harper's Ferry, while Gen. Longstreet proceeded on to Hagerstown. Gen. Miles, the Federal commander, with twelve thousand troops, occupied Harper's Ferry. The Federals, learning of Gen. Longstreet's movements, turned their force to the gap in the mountain. As a counter movement Gen. Lee had placed Gen. D. H. Hill on the other side of the gap with part of his forces occupying the top, with instructions to hold his position until Gen. Jackson's success was assured. To understand the relative position of these two great armies and the nature of the battle that followed, a description of this pass is necessary, and certainly will be interesting to the reader. "The road is winding, narrow, rocky, and rugged, with either a deep ravine on one side and the steep side of the mountain on the other, or like a huge channel cut through a solid rock. Near the crest are three houses which overlook the valley, but elsewhere the face of the mountain is unbroken by a solitary habitation."

At the dawn of day an artillery duel of two hours' duration opened the battle, which was then taken up along the whole line. The overpowering numbers seemed for a while to compel a retreat of the Confederates. Gen. Longstreet, with fresh troops and with his rally cry, made the boys in blue more determined not to yield with a tenacity equal to those who wore the gray. Though outnumbered five times, the Confederates held their position until darkness brought a needed rest to man and beast. Jackson claimed the victory.

Surrender of Harper's Ferry.

September 14 Gen. Jackson hurled his volleys of

death upon the whole Federal lines and fortifications. The hoisting of a flag of truce surrendered eleven thousand troops, seventy-three pieces of artillery, and two hundred wagons. Their brave commander, Gen. Miles, had his left thigh shot away. Once again Jackson's ragged boys caused the surrender of a magnificently equipped army, blessed with everything that could be necessary to complete equipment and to make a soldier happy.

Battle of Sharpsburg.

Gen. Lee had now determined to confront the advancing force of McClellan in possession of Crampton's Gap, on the road from Frederick City to Sharpsburg, the latter place being about ten miles from Harper's Ferry, resting in a deep valley in the midst of a rugged and broken country. September 17 he settled his forty-five thousand men in a strong position, when he was attacked by Gen. McClellan, who commanded in person a force of one hundred and fifty thousand finely trained men, with the following divisions: Gens. Burnside, McDowell, Hooker, Sumner, Franklin, Williams, and Sykes. The line of battle of this great army extended over five miles. Tuesday evening (16th) the Federal batteries prepared the Confederates for an early renewal the next morning. At daybreak the battle was opened and continued by the pickets until it merged into a general engagement. "The Federals advanced between Antietam and the Sharpsburg and Hagerstown turnpike, and were met by Gen. D. H. Hill and Gen. Longstreet, where the conflict raged, extending on the Confederate left." The mortality among the Federals was terrible, for they were in a position where the guns of the Confederates were used against them with such telling effect that they fell as grain falls before the blade of the reapers; consequently, after a stubborn contest and fighting as never men fought before, they were forced to fall back. The Confederates nearest where the Federals crossed the Potomac were on the point of being overwhelmed, when the divisions of Gens. McLaws, Anderson, and Walker came to their assistance. With these new troops the ranks were restored, and they held their position.

To give the testimony of a Federal officer: "It is beyond all comprehension how men such as the Rebel troops are can fight as they do. That those ragged wretches—sick, hungry, and tired—should prove such heroes in battle is beyond explanation. Men never fought better. There was one regiment that stood up before the fire of two or three of our long-range batteries and two regiments of infantry, and though the air around them was vocal with the whistle of the bullets and the scream of the shells, there they stood and delivered their fire in perfect order."

In the afternoon the Federals made a vain attack upon the Confederate right, which was held by Gen. Jones; but they met with better success in forcing Gen. Toombs, of Georgia, from his position at the bridge over Antietam Creek. Gen. A. P. Hill came with reënforcements, thus swelling the number to seventy thousand. After nightfall, with ammunition exhausted, both sides had to content themselves with a drawn battle, each side retaining the same position in which it had begun the conflict. On both sides the loss was about the same—estimated between five and nine thousand. The Federals left during the night, while Gen. Lee took position at Shepherdstown. On the 20th the Federals made a pretense of attacking him at this point, but were caused to retreat by Gen. A. P. Hill. The repulse time and again of the two glorious armies who wore the blue and the gray will give renown of brilliant courage handed down to our children as a military achievement almost without a parallel.

CHAPTER XI.

MOVEMENTS IN THE WEST AGAIN.

The North had arranged a programme of operations in the country west of the Alleghanies. These preparations surpassed in magnitude all military movements which had been designed or attempted since the beginning of the war, the main object being the expulsion of all Confederates from Kentucky, Tennessee, and the States west of the Mississippi river, and also the penetration through the Gulf States. The Federals were at this time on their way into all these places, while another army was operating in Missouri and Arkansas. Also there was on the waters of the Misissippi a fleet of gunboats which was considered impregnable in strength.

Nothing was now left for the South to do but to make a forward movement, by which North Alabama and Middle and East Tennessee should be relieved, and the Federals forced to fall back, and assistance given to Gen. Buell, who was at this time in Kentucky. The brief retirement of the favorite Gen. Beauregard, on account of ill health, was a misfortune to the Confederates. Gen. Braxton Bragg took his place. The first step of this aggressive movement was the ordering of Gen. Kirby Smith to advance into Kentucky and threaten Cincinnati, the main object being to force the Federals across the Ohio river.

Early in the month of August Gen. McCown moved his division from London to Knoxville; thence the

Confederates moved to the gap in the Cumberland Mountains, being joined by Gen. Cleburne at the lower gap, when the whole force—with baggage, trains, and artillery—were ordered through. They then made a forced march until they reached Barboursville. Halting there a few hours to rest their wearied limbs, they pushed rapidly on to Cumberland Ford, and were there given several days of much needed rest.

August 29 Gen. Kirby Smith found the Federals near Richmond, Ky., and determined to march against them. The leading division, under Gen. Cleburne, after advancing three miles, found the Federals drawn up in line of battle in a fine position near Mt. Zion Church, six miles from Richmond, Ky. Without waiting for Gen. Churchill's troops, he at once commenced action, firing very briskly. Gen. Churchill was sent to turn the Federals' right, which he succeeded in doing admirably. At the same time the Federals made an attempt to flank Gen. Cleburne's right, but were thwarted by the gallant charge of Col. Preston Smith's Brigade, which repulsed them with great slaughter. Gen. Smith then ordered the cavalry to proceed to the north of Richmond in order to cut off the retreat of the Federals. The Confederate artillerymen having ceased their firing, the Federals, thinking the silence of their guns meant a retreat, made an attack upon the Texas and Arkansas troops under McCray, who met them and fought the battle alone, and by courageous charging upon their advancing lines forced a retreat. The wildest confusion was witnessed, "leaving knapsacks, swords, pistols, hats, and canteens scattered along the roadside, where their dead and dying too plainly showed the way."

Gen. Smith received information that Gen. Nelson had arrived with reënforcements, and therefore determined to make a stand on a commanding ridge. Gens. Churchill and Preston Smith, at double-quick, formed in front of Gen. Nelson's center and left. The Confederates advanced under destructive fire from twice their number, and forced the retreat of the Federals. The worn-out, exhausted condition of the Southern soldiers and the darkness of the night prevented a further pursuit of the Federals. The results of the day added new glories to the Southern arms.

September 4 Gen. Preston Smith, with forces consisting of a Texas and an Arkansas brigade, under command of Gen. Churchill, and Gens. Cleburne's and Heath's Divisions—all being under the command of Gen. Kirby Smith—was welcomed into the beautiful city of Lexington, Ky.

"The entrance of Confederate troops into Lexington was the occasion of the most inspiring and touching scenes. Streets, windows, and gardens were filled with ladies and little girls with streams of red and blue ribbon and flags with stars and bars upon them. Private residences were turned into public houses of entertainment free to all who could be persuaded to go and partake of the feast with the boys in gray on Kentucky's hallowed soil."

Many were expecting Gen. Smith to capture Cincinnati, but his orders were to menace, not attack. Consequently his orders were to fall back and coöperate with the army under Gen. Bragg, who had entered the State by the eastern route, crossing the Cumberland River at Gainesboro, with the design of flanking Gen. Buell. Gen. Smith's movements were soon discovered by Gen. Nelson. September 17 Gen. Bragg captured five thousand Federals at Munfordville, Ky., with a very small loss on the Confederate side, and on October 4 joined Gen. Kirby Smith at Frankfort, Ky.

Battle of Perryville, October 8.

By harassing his rear near Perryville the Federals showed Gen. Bragg that they were desirous for a fight, he having only fifteen thousand soldiers against forty-five thousand of the splendidly equipped army of United States soldiers. About midday the battle opened, with Gen. Hardee commanding Buckner's and Anderson's Divisions on the left, and Gen. Polk with Cheatham's and Withers' Divisions on the right. Col. Powell's Brigade, on the extreme left, succeeded in pushing back for over a mile the largely superior numbers opposed to him. Gen. Adams' Brigade, after holding the position for three hours, retreated with a loss of a large number of men. When night put an end to this hotly contested engagement of the boys who wore the blue and the gray, bravely contested by both sides, the Federal loss was four thousand killed and wounded, seven thousand prisoners, and fifteen pieces of artillery; while the Confederate loss, in killed, wounded, and missing, was twenty-five hundred.

Just as at Shiloh, the Confederates lost by overpowering numbers. As the shades of night fell upon the battle of Perryville, Ky., after desperate fighting on both sides, such as men never fought before, a weak point, held sternly by Gen. George Maney's Brigade of Tennesseeans under command of the gallant Col. Fields, was attacked. Gen. Polk, seeing the situation, waved his hat and sword at different times and said: "Tennesseeans, retake that battery." Lieut. Col. Patterson, with hat lifted high over his head, called to his men: "Follow me, boys." It was a charge to death for that brave young officer. Maj. Kelly, with a courage equal to inspiration, headed the charge as they marched to victory.

Among other deeds of heroism, many of which were performed by young boys, we know of Johnnie Carter, sergeant, a son of Dan F. Carter, of Nashville, Tenn., one who is well remembered. A desperate hand to hand fight was going on. These brave boys plunged into the jaws of death in the most heroic manner. Johnnie (Serg. John Carter) grasped his flagstaff. When found he was firmly holding his flag, seeming loath to give it up. Little did the brave boy dream a mortal wound had struck him. Leaving a home of luxury, an only boy of doting parents, an only brother of a loving sister, Johnnie laid his young life on the altar of his country. His beloved surgeon, Dr. J. R. Buist, and his loving parents were with him, ministering tenderly to his every want and comfort.

BATTLE OF CORINTH.

Having united the forces of Gen. Price with his own, on Friday, October 3, Gen. Van Dorn prepared to attack the Federals fortified at Corinth. His forces, consisting of only one division commanded by Gen. Lovell, held the right, the extreme positions on the

Destruction of Cotton at the Taking of New Orleans. (See page 46.)

Harper's Ferry. (See page 60.)

left and right being occupied by Gens. Herbert and Maney respectively.

The battle began at seven o'clock by Gen. Villipigue's Battery opening a severe fire upon the Federals, which forced them to make a gradual retreat for two hours. Here, within half a mile of their line of fortifications, the Federals made a stubborn stand. The whole Confederate line now moved grandly forward to the attack. In the midst of one of the grandest fires from the Federal batteries these boys in gray advanced in double-quick charge, forcing the boys in blue from their first to their second line of intrenchments. Here the battle ended for that day.

Gen. Van Dorn, overconfident and ignorant of the strength of the army before him, telegraphed to Richmond the news of the victory.

The next morning the conflict was renewed. The Federals, with heroic courage, received the terrific artillery fire, which was kept up until ten o'clock, when the whole line advanced again. Nothing could withstand them. But in the very enthusiasm of victory, inspired by the spirit of battle itself, the individual soldier forgot order (on both sides), and in the greatest and wildest confusion they plunged. Here the Federals turned loose their batteries, and either a retreat or the taking of the Federal battery on College Hill was inevitable. The latter course was ordered. Eight deep, in grim and determined silence, these brave men advanced almost in the very jaws of death itself, in the face of bullets as thick as raindrops in a summer shower. Still advancing, and falling by the hundreds, they reached the top of the hill. Twice were they beaten back, but the third time they seemed to succeed. A cheer was raised above the din of battle, and the Southern cross, with stars and bars, floated to the breeze in the place of the United States flag; but it was immediately torn away. Again it was set up, and the old flag pulled down again, but only to be shot to pieces. Physical nature inspired by divine courage could do no more. The bleeding, shattered ranks, after giving an exhibition of fortitude that glorifies the human race, fell back, followed by an increased fire from the Federals at close range, and the day was lost. But even then they were unwilling to give up the contest without another struggle, and retired to the shelter of the woods to await the expected attack of the Federals; but the latter seemed worn out and contented with the day's fighting. Consequently Gen. Van Dorn began to withdraw his forces.

Next morning he was again attacked, which produced temporary confusion, but order was soon restored, and an artillery fire was kept up all day. Gen. Van Dorn gradually led his troops across the Hatchie river, and took a position near Ripley. In killed, wounded, and prisoners, Gen. Van Dorn lost forty-five hundred men, while the Federals lost about half that number.

Guerrilla Warfare in Missouri.

The State of Missouri had much to complain of. From one end of her borders to the other she had been overrun with the full license of war—robbery, murder, and pillage being the order of the day. Consequently, as a matter of self-defense, and to protect themselves against such, the citizens began to organize themselves into irregular bands known as "guerrillas." Troops of this character, however, did not disdain to try conclusions with the Federals in open battle. August 6 Porter's band was attacked by a large force of Federals under Col. McNeil, at Kirksville, and retreated after a battle, killing fully one thousand Federals and losing five hundred men. On the 15th of August the same was followed by a total defeat of the Federals near Lone Jack by Hughes's and Quantrell's bands, only the arrival of reënforcements saving the Federals from destruction.

CHAPTER XII.

CAMPAIGN IN NORTHERN VIRGINIA.

Nor satisfied with the slow movements of Gen. McClellan, the Federal government superseded him with Gen. Burnside. He began operations by massing his forces at Fredericksburg, Va., with the determination of crossing the Rappahannock. Consequently on December 10 he began to construct three bridges over the Rappahannock: "two at Fredericksburg, and a third about a mile and a quarter below Deep Run. The Federals were defended by their artillery on the hills of Stafford, which completely commanded the plain upon which Fredericksburg stands." During the process of construction the Seventeenth Mississippi Regiment of Barksdale Brigade, posted on the bluffs on the opposite side of the river, opened fire on the Federals, which was grandly replied to with a storm of shells. Though the Confederates harassed the Federals persistently and incessantly all through the night, they succeeded in finishing their bridges. The Confederates retreated through the streets of Fredericksburg, followed by heavy fire from the Federals, which forced the citizens to evacuate the city and to flee to the surrounding country for protection. By the 13th the Confederates had taken a strong position upon the bluffs on the south bank of the river, presenting to the Federals a front six miles in length. Twelve o'clock in the day the Federals moved across the valley intervening between Confederate forces and theirs. Gen. Stuart's Horse Artillery gave a terrible cannonading, but the Federals managed to keep on across the valley until they came within protection of the woods, from which position they were driven by Gens. Hill's and Early's troops, and pursued until they reached the shelter of their batteries. While this portion of the Confederate line, which consisted of Jackson's Corps, was thus engaged, the Federals also advanced against Gen. Longstreet's position on the left, and directed their principal attack against Mayre's Hill, upon which were stationed the Washington Artillery, of New Orleans, and a part of McLaw's Division. Right gallantly did the boys in gray press to the charge, facing the terrific fire of shot and shell turned upon them with such effectiveness as to make the ground over which they passed literally a ghastly field of dead men. Broken and shattered, the boys in blue reeled back into the town, when night put an end to the conflict. The pale December moon gave a ghastlier appearance to a field already horrible in the extreme. The tenacity with which each side fought was shown in the number of killed, for the field is said to have been literally strewn with dead. At the foot of Mayre's Hill was a frightful carnage. The victory was indeed a costly one to the Confederates. The number of killed and wounded signified much to them: it meant a vacant place in their ranks which could not be filled; a gap which, when closed up, brought the wings closer together. Consequently the fruits of the victory at Fredericksburg hardly compensated for the loss they had sustained, which was eighteen hundred, among whom were Gens. Cobb, of Georgia, and Gregg, of South Carolina.

The Federal loss in killed, wounded, and missing, was ten thousand. Gen. Burnside crossed the Rappahannock safely with his shattered army.

While narrating the story of man's stern devotion to duty on the bloody field of carnage, woman's quieter, though none the less noble, devotion we cannot pass over. Therefore, in quoting the language of a historian in regard to the women of Fredericksburg during this time, one but describes the women of the whole South during the shifting and trying scenes of the civil war:

> The romance of the story of Fredericksburg is written no less in the quiet heroism of her women than in deeds of arms. The verses of a poet, rather than the cold language of a mere chronicler of events, are more befitting to describe the beautiful and noble sacrifices of those brave daughters of Virginia. In all the terrible scenes of Fredericksburg there were no weaknesses and tears of women. Mothers, exiles from home, met their sons in the ranks, embraced them, told them to do their duty, and, with a self-negation most touching to witness, concealed their wants, sometimes their hunger, telling their brave boys that they were comfortable and happy. At Hamilton's Crossing many of the women met relatives in the army. No more touching and noble evidence could be offered of the heroism of the women of Fredericksburg than the gratitude of the army. When subscriptions for their relief came to be added up, it was found that thousands of dollars had been contributed by the soldier boys to the refugee fund. There could be no more eloquent tribute offered than this—a beautiful and immortal souvenir of their sufferings and virtue.

THE FEDERALS IN NORTH CAROLINA.

During the month of December the Federal army was actively engaged in overrunning the State of North Carolina. Near Kinston Gen. Evans, with two thousand men, succeeded in holding them in check for three days, from the 13th to the 16th. The Federal army consisted of fifteen thousand, commanded by Gen. Foster. They then moved against Gen. Robertson at Whitehall Bridge, over the Neuse river, eighteen miles below Goldsboro. They were forced to retreat with great loss. This was followed by an attack of the whole Confederate force—under Gens. Evans, Clingman, and Pettigrew—upon the Federal position along the river (Neuse). The Federals retreated to their fortifications and gunboats with a loss of three hundred in killed and wounded. The Confederates had held the Federals in check, and had prevented them from accomplishing anything of special importance.

GEN. HINDMAN'S SUCCESS IN ARKANSAS.

Before closing the record in our narrative of 1862 Gen. Hindman's encounter with the Federals on the 27th of November, at Prairie Grove, Ark., must be related. With nine thousand men, Gen. Hindman sustained himself against a double force, the Federals making stubborn charges upon his lines. When the day ended Gen. Hindman had pushed the Federals back, with a loss of one thousand killed and wounded, three hundred prisoners, and a large amount of stores. The total Confederate loss was three hundred.

CAVALRY EXPLOITS.

On the other side of the Mississippi River the last movements of the year were signalized by Confederate cavalry raids under Gens. Forrest, Morgan, and Clarkson, by which the Federals were greatly harassed, for they never knew where these hard riders, with their gray jackets, would strike a blow. When they thought they had them, with guns ready to fire, these raiders would vanish like a shadow. On December 7 Gen. John Morgan, around whose name the glamour of a romantic story has spread itself, succeeded in taking the town of Hartsville, Tenn., on the Cumberland River, near Nashville, Tenn., finding there two thousand stands of arms, a large quantity of provisions, two pieces of artillery, and eighteen hundred prisoners. This exploit was followed by Col. Clarkson with like success, taking Piketon, Ky.

The year 1862 had been a brilliant one to Southern soldiers, though overshadowed by many disasters, with glorious victories for the Federals. The story of the successive battles has given to the world a proof of the devotion of the troops of the North and South, and, with the record before them, both sides are vigorously preparing to enter a new year. Gen. Pemberton was appointed to supersede Gen. Van Dorn at Holly Springs. Gen. Joseph E. Johnston was put in command of all the armies between the mountains and the great river, and Gen. Beauregard was ordered to defend the cities of Charleston and Savannah against a large fleet being prepared by the Federals.

CHAPTER XIII.

MURFREESBORO—GALVESTON—ARKANSAS POST.

At Murfreesboro, Tenn., Gen. Braxton Bragg had concentrated an army of thirty thousand in number, coming principally from the extreme Southern States—Louisiana, Florida, South Carolina, Mississippi, Alabama, Georgia, Kentucky, and Tennessee. The horrors of battle were not new to these boys who wore the gray, for they were the same ones who had given evidence of such magnificent courage and endurance at Shiloh, Perryville, and other less memorable fields of battle. They were here resting from the dread alarms of war, and had entered with all a soldier's zest into the full enjoyment of the festivities of Christmas, when, on Friday, December 26, word was brought from Nashville that Gen. Rosecrans was marching against them with an army of over forty thousand soldiers, being one of the finest equipped, and commanded by the bravest officers.

The scene changes from the pleasure of the ballroom to the sterner duties alloted them as soldiers.

The grounds had been surveyed and examined to select a position for battle in case of a surprise, and the Confederates were thrown forward to prevent one, ready to meet their elegantly equipped friends in their suits of blue. Polk's Corps, with Cheatham's Division, occupied the center; Maney's Brigade was thrown forward toward LaVergne, where Wheeler's Cavalry was giving great trouble to Gen.

Rosecrans; a portion of Gen. Kirby Smith's Corps, McCown's Division, occupied Readyville, on the Confederate right, and Hardee's Corps Triune, on the left. The Confederates arranged in line of battle on the 28th, with Polk's, Cheatham's, and Withers' Divisions on the west bank of Stone's River, with a front six miles long, which rested respectively on the Nashville and Salem pikes. Hardee's Corps and Breckinridge's and Cleburne's Divisions held a position on the east bank of the river, stretching over a distance of three miles, thus making the whole line nine miles, in the shape of an obtuse angle. McCown's Division and Gen. Jackson's Brigade were held as reserves for the center and right flank respectively. After skirmishing and cannonading on the 29th and the morning of the 30th, the Federals massed their forces and attacked the Confederate left, charging Robinson's Battery no less than three times; but each time were met by the Tennesseeans, the One Hundred and Fifty-Fourth Regiment. To prevent concentration against the left Gens. McCown's and Cleburne's Divisions were moved to meet them. In the meantime Gen. Wheeler's Cavalry had given the Federals a great surprise, capturing a large wagon train and many prisoners. Although this cold December night chilled the boys of both armies alike as they sat around the camp fires, their ardor was not dampened. The last day of the month the charge was begun by Cleburne's and McCown's Divisions, and gave the Federals a great surprise. The bright sun broke through the clouds just at this time, shedding a ray of splendor upon that gray column as it moved forward, the Federals retreating six miles. Withers' and Cheatham's

Divisions had an encounter, and it is said, from the number of dead and the batteries left behind, that the blow to the Federals was heavy. It is related that the charge, " like a hurricane scattering leaves in its course," literally blackened the ground with the dead for miles, as on they swept, through fields and ravines and over ditches and fences.

The Confederates had taken nearly five thousand prisoners, thirty pieces of artillery, five thousand stands of arms, and a large amount of ammunition.

Gen. Rosecrans had made a fatal mistake by weakening his left and center, and the Confederates took advantage it. Consequently, unperceived by the Confederates, he moved his center forward and took a strong position on the hill. This the Confederates charged, with immense numbers opposing them, but were forced to fall back. They camped the night, New Year's, 1863, in the midst of the dead and wounded. Gen. Bragg presented a glorious victory to Richmond authorities, but, unfortunately, the Federals were allowed to restore order among their disorganized forces, having a strong position in the bend of the river, which Gen. Breckinridge was ordered to take. At four o'clock the order to move was given, and the fated band moved forward like the very embodiment of courage to that awful charge, in the face of such a storm of artillery and musketry as was never displayed on any battlefield. The Federals retreated from the ridge to the river. The Twentieth Tennessee Regiment captured two hundred prisoners. They next turned their attention to those on the other side of the river. They crossed in the midst of such a fire that in a short space of time two thousand vacant places were made in the homes of the South. The sacrifice seemed useless to both sides, only as an example of good courage that causes one to honor his race the more as he reads the narrative. Gens. Chalmers and Donelson, supported by Gen. Wheeler's Brigade and Maney's Brigade of Tennesseeans, faced the fire from the hill. Gen. W. H. Jackson, of Nashville, crossed the river to relieve the broken columns. Gen. Wheeler flanked the Federals' rear, with the assistance of Gen. Wharton, capturing sixteen hundred wagons and three thousand mules. Gens. Hanson and Palmer formed the first line to attack him in his stronghold; Gen. Pillow on the right; Gens. Hunt, Preston, and Gibson, the second line in the rear. These brave boys charged with fury, and carried the ridge with a yell, and the Federals retreated. Capt. Wright placed his battery on the very top of the hill, sending sheets of flame down into the river. He was mortally wounded. Gen. James Rains also fell while gallantly leading his men. Gen. Hanson, of Kentucky, who had a brother in the Federal army, gave up his life. His last words were: "I am willing to die with such a wound, received in so glorious a cause." With these heroic words he joined those who had also fallen for the same cause. Col. Marks lost his leg, and Capt. L. N. Savage lost his life—both noble Tennesseeans.

On the next day (Jan. 3) Gen. Bragg withdrew his army to Tullahoma, while the Federal forces occupied Murfreesboro. This battle was accounted a Federal success, in that the Confederates did not hold their position. The loss in killed and wounded was greater on the Federal side than on the Confederate.

Capture of Galveston.

As an offset to the partial disaster at Murfreesboro, the Confederates began the new year with a victory at Galveston, Tex. On the morning of December 31 Gen. Magruder, with seven regiments of infantry and twenty-two guns, proceeded to retake the city, which, as has been noticed in a previous chapter, had been captured by the Federals. Only a few of the latter, however, occupied the city; but out in the harbor, not three hundred yards from the shore, lay five Federal gunboats with their guns ready, and frowning threateningly upon the city of Galveston. Silently Gen. Magruder's little band moved through the streets, and took position on Strand Street near the wharves; and before daylight he astonished the citizens with a roar of his guns directed against the great ships. It soon became evident that the small Confederate battery was no match for their heavy guns. An attack was made on the Forty-Second Massachusetts Regiment, which was fortified at one end of the wharf.

Assistance now came to the Confederates from the water. The Bayou City, the Neptune, the John F. Can, and the Lucy Gwinn steamed toward the Federal vessels, directing their attention especially to the Harriet Lane, which the Neptune struck amidships, and, having cleared her decks by fire from small arms, the crew of the latter were preparing to board the Lane when it was discovered that their own vessel was damaged to such an extent as to be sinking; consequently they steamed off and sunk her. The Bayou City next attacked the Federal vessel, and boarded her and forced a surrender. The other ships managed to escape out of the harbor, with the exception of the Westfield, which was burned.

Surrender of Arkansas Post.

On January 11, after two days' attack with both water and land forces, the Federals under Gen. MacClernand succeeded in forcing the surrender of Arkansas Post, on the Arkansas river, which was held by Gen. Churchill with over three thousand troops. This victory was important to the Federals, in that it gave them control of the Arkansas river.

Confederate Rams Attack the Federals in Charleston Harbor.

In Charleston Harbor, on January 30, the Confederate rams moved out against the Federal fleet, which had held a position off the mouth of the harbor for over a month. The result of this attack was the disabling of the Mercedita and the Keystone State, the latter losing twenty-one men.

The Federal gunboat Queen of the West had passed the Confederate batteries at Vicksburg, and was committing depredations on Red River. She had also captured a small Confederate boat, the Era. The commander of the Queen of the West had forced the pilot of the Era, George Wood, to take the helm of the Queen of the West and direct her toward the capture of a Confederate fort on the river. Wood drove her ashore just opposite the fort, however, and turned her side to the batteries, and in the confusion which followed from this movement succeeded in making his escape. Part of the crew of the Queen of the West, and her commander, jumped

Destruction of the Hatteras by the Confederate Steamer Alabama.

The Sumter Running the Blockade, and Chased by the Federal Ship Iroquois.

upon cotton bales and floated down the river; but the remainder, thirteen in number, remained on board all night, and the next morning the Confederates took possession. In like manner another Federal vessel, the Indianola, passed the Confederate batteries, and for some time was a great annoyance. Consequently the Queen of the West, the Webb, the Era, and the Dr. Batey, under command of Maj. Walker, went in quest of the Federal gunboat. On February 24 the Confederates moved to the attack, and after a terrible contest of over an hour's duration it was found that the Indianola was in a sinking condition. Her officers surrendered with her crew of one hundred and twenty men.

While the Confederates were gaining these successes on the inland waters, they also had a few privateers upon the Atlantic ocean, which were doing great damage to Federal shipping, and the exploits of the Florida and Alabama were such as even to call forth praise from the North.

CHAPTER XIV.

IMPRESSMENT—BATTERIES AND GUNBOATS.

BEFORE again taking up the thread of military operations, it is right to notice briefly the law of impressment, which the Confederate Congress was forced to enact on account of a scarcity of provisions. The great grain-producing districts had all felt the iron heel of war; and the State of Kentucky, which had heretofore furnished the principal supply of meat to the army, was now in the hands of the Federal government. Moreover, the paper money of the Confederacy, with no assurance back of it save a promise to pay six months after the close of the war, had been turned loose upon the country to such an extent that in the beginning of the year 1863 there was $300,000,000 in circulation. Consequently it had so decreased in value that one dollar in silver was worth four dollars in paper. With the scarcity of food and the depreciated value of the currency, the South was cursed with the misfortune of speculation. Therefore, without discussing the nature of such matters, it was plain what the ultimate results and effects would be.

FEDERALS ATTACK FORT McALLISTER.

On March 3 the Federals made an attack with five vessels upon Fort McAllister, on the Ogeechee river, near Savannah, Ga. All day they bombarded the fort, but at night they withdrew with one of their ironclads badly damaged, while the fort had only one gun dismounted, and within its walls not a single life was lost.

The Federals in Front of Vicksburg.

The Federals had three objects in view to obtain the capture of Vicksburg: First, the canal across the isthmus opposite the city; secondly, the project of getting through the Yazoo Pass; thirdly, the Lake Providence Canal project. All this time it had been their object to get in the rear of Vicksburg. Their present plan was to get through the Yazoo Pass, in hope of cutting off Confederate supplies. The idea was to flank Vicksburg, capture Jackson, cut off Grenada, and thereby destroy all possibility of getting supplies from that immensely rich country.

On March 13 they began active operations by an attack with their gunboats on that part of the Confederate works known as Fort Pemberton, situated in the bend of the Tallahatchie river. After four hours of heavy fighting in front of Vicksburg, the Federals were forced to retire. This defeat produced a lull in the operations of the Federals in the immediate vicinity of Vicksburg. They next turned their attention to Port Hudson, "a strongly fortified position on the lower Mississippi, about sixteen miles above Baton Rouge, and three hundred below Vicksburg." Accordingly, six magnificent ships were fitted out, under command of Admiral Farragut, a distinguished naval officer of the United States navy. They attempted to pass the batteries, which were located on a high bluff. Silently these mighty war monsters passed on, with each man waiting intently at his gun; but they were discovered when just opposite the batteries, and the alarm was given. Immediately the ships opened the thunders of their artillery upon the Confederates, who endured the fire in silence until they all got within easy range, when they let loose such a storm of shot and shell upon the Federals that it soon became plain that it meant destruction for the ships to pass. Therefore all except the Hartford turned around and steamed back in the midst of a fire that furnished a grand scene as shell after shell cut its bright way through the darkness of the night. All managed to escape injury except the Mississippi, whose rudder was broken and so injured that she floated aimlessly to the opposite shore, giving the batteries a good opportunity to tear her literally to pieces. Most of her crew succeeded in escaping, but the wounded were left on board the vessel, which floated off down the river, and when near Baton Rouge her magazine exploded, sending to the bottom of the big Mississippi river one of the most magnificent ships of the United States navy.

During these engagements both armies in Virginia and Tennessee, the boys in blue and gray, were watching each other without any apparent movement on either side. But the monotony was somewhat broken by a force of Federals three thousand strong crossing the Rappahannock river at Kelly's Ford March 17. They continued their march until within six miles of Culpepper C. H., when they were attacked by Gen. Fitzhugh Lee's Brigade. After several hours' hard fighting they retreated. The Confederates lost in killed and wounded about one hundred men, among whom was the youthful and gallant Maj. Pelham, of

Alabama, who, although but twenty-two years of age, had been through all the battles in Virginia, and had won that enduring fame and honor which only comes to men after long experience and services of many years. Peace be to the ashes of this "boy major!" and may the roses of immortality ever bloom over his grave, inasmuch as he typified in his own person and death all of that fresh, glorious young manhood of the South that went down in that awful struggle, even though they wore not upon their shoulders the straps of rank and lie in nameless graves!

The Federals Repulsed from Charleston.

To the minds of the Federals Charleston, S. C., was "the cradle of the rebellion." Therefore its capture was considered one of great importance. The known design of the Federals had kept the citizens of Charleston in a state of suspense. On April 7, when a part of the Federal fleet, which consisted of more than seventy vessels, moved to attack Fort Sumter, when in the midst of the strains of "Dixie," the iron throats of the cannon spoke forth their volleys of death and destruction. The fleet advanced in two divisions, led respectively by the ironclads Ironsides and Keokuk, which delivered a tremendous fire upon the walls of both Forts Sumter and Morris, and in return they received a crushing tempest of iron hail from the heavy guns of the two forts, so that they were forced to withdraw out of range. So effective was the fire under Gen. Beauregard that it was discovered that the Keokuk was sunk near Morris Island. The Confederates lost only one man killed and five wounded.

CHAPTER XV.

CHANCELLORSVILLE—VICKSBURG—GETTYSBURG.

It now became Gen. Hooker's turn to try the fortunes of war with Gen. Robert E. Lee. Accordingly, with an army which he himself said was "the finest on the planet," on April 26, he began the crossing of the Rappahannock in three large divisions. One was to cross at Kelly's Ford; another at Deep Run, three miles below Fredericksburg; and a third at United States Ford, "just below the confluence of the Rappahannock and Rapidan." By Thursday, April 29, Gen. Hooker had accomplished all of these movements, and had fortified himself in a strong position "across the turnpike and plank road at Chancellorsville, eleven miles from Fredericksburg, in order to cut off the Confederates' anticipated retreat in the direction of Gordonsville." Gen. Lee soon discovered that the Federals had crossed the river at Kelly's and Ellis' Fords. Gen. Wright's Brigade was ordered to support the Confederate forces, eight thousand in number, under Gen. Anderson, Posey and Mahone guarding the approaches to Fredericksburg in that direction. During the night of April 29 Gen. Lee himself, with Anderson's and McLaw's Divisions, took a position in front of the Federals, while he sent Gen. Jackson to get in their rear. This skillful movement was successfully accomplished by May 2, when Gen. Jackson hurled his veterans against the Federals' right and rear. Gen. Sigel's Corps of Germans

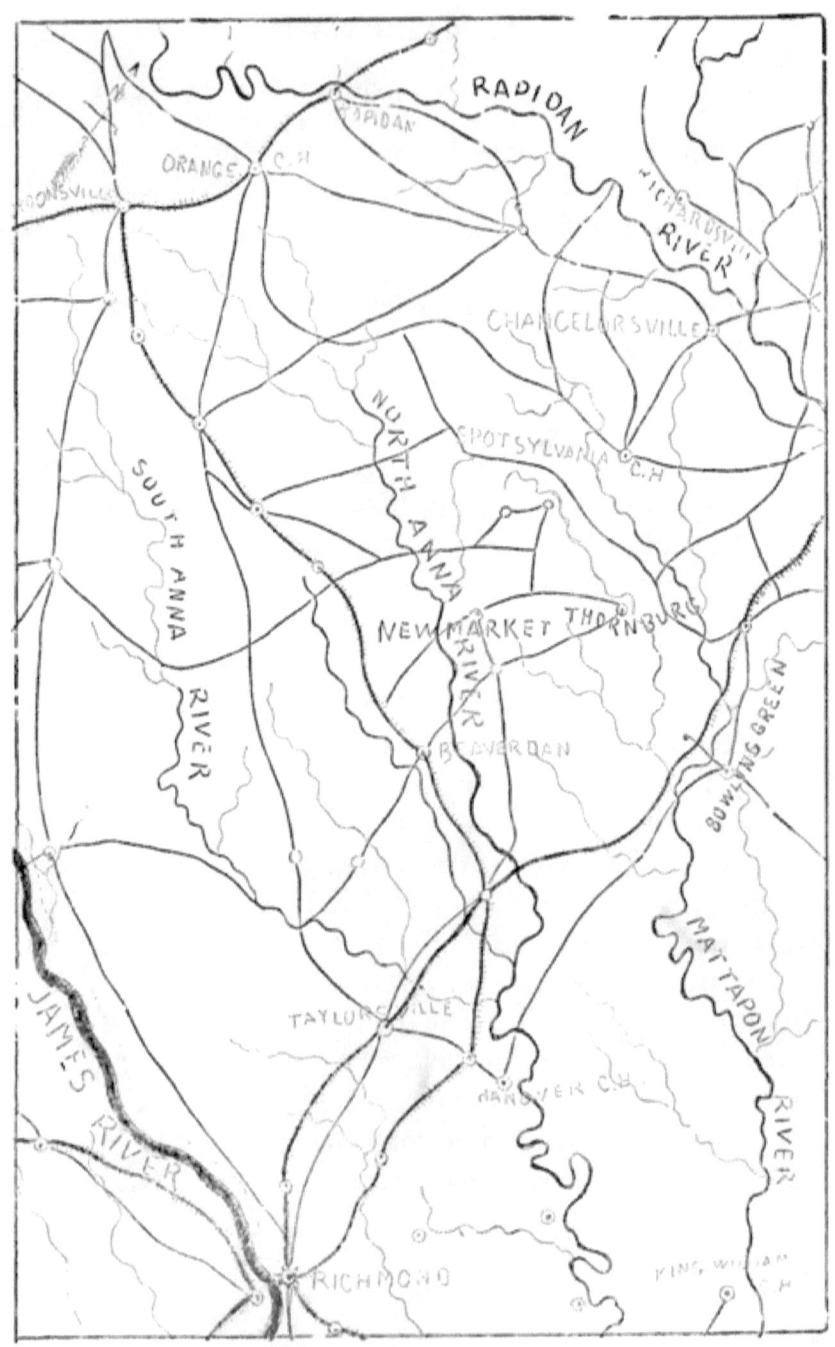

Map of Northern Virginia.

was the unfortunate portion of the Federal army that received Gen. Jackson's charge, which threw them in confusion upon the guns of Gens. Anderson's and McLaw's Divisions, and they retreated toward the river. There was now a lull in the battle. Gen. Stuart took command, Gens. Jackson and Hill both having been wounded. In accordance with instructions from the former, Gen. Stuart continued to batter the Federals' right wing. For a while they rested, these old veterans, the blue and the gray. Sunday morning the battle was renewed by the Confederates making a charge upon the fortifications and rifle pits of the Federals. The Confederates now seemed to be on the point of a great victory, and Gen. Lee moved his forces to the plank road above Chancellorsville. But while thus successful in this portion of their lines, the Confederates were defeated at Fredericksburg, where Barksdale's Brigade and Early's Division held a position extending from Mayre's Hill to Hamilton's Crossing. With two thousand troops, the Washington Artillery, of New Orleans, and Read's Battery, stationed on a hill, Gen. Barksdale occupied the left. Against these small numbers the Federals hurled with great force Sedgewick's Corps, twenty thousand strong. Three times did they throw the weight of their immense numbers upon the brave little band on the heights, and each time they were sent back broken in ranks, with their dead lying thick on the hillside. Hearing of this reverse, Gen. Lee turned his attention from Hooker, and sent Anderson's and McLaw's Divisions to stop Gen. Sedgewick, which they succeeded in doing, when night put an end to the contest.

The next day the Federals prepared to renew the attack by concentrating their forces against the left flank of Gen. McLaw's Division. Gen. Lee at once took advantage by massing Anderson's and Early's Divisions at this point. But it was not the purpose of Gen. Lee to let the contest end here, and he began the disposition of his troops so as to completely destroy the army of Gen. Hooker. A violent rainstorm set in, which caused a lull in Gen. Lee's operations, the Federals retreating across the river during the storm.

To sum up the fruits of the victory, an army of fifty thousand had met an army "variously estimated at from one hundred thousand to one hundred and fifty thousand." The Confederates had taken large amounts of supplies, seven thousand prisoners, and four thousand stands of arms. The Federals lost twenty-five thousand in killed and wounded. To the Confederate soldiers the laurels of Chancellorsville will ever be draped in the sable hue of mourning for their ideal leader—great among the earth's great captains—who laid down his command to enlist in that immortal army where battles and wars are no more. Gen. Stonewall Jackson, at eight o'clock Saturday, May 2, while returning to his line, received three balls in his arm, which was amputated, finally causing his death. With his beloved wife and loved ones around him, he passed away, his last words being: "Let us cross over the river, and rest under the shade of the trees."

Battle of Raymond, Miss.

After a weary march of two hundred miles from

Port Hudson, Gen. John Gregg, of Texas, pitched his tent one mile north of Jackson, Miss. Gen. Grierson, of the Federal army, had torn up the railroad, hence the march for those poor boys on foot. The Tennessee soldiers, though worn out and weary physically, were a jubilant set of men, feeling they were homeward bound. Gen. Gregg's Brigade was composed of the Forty-First Tennessee, Col. Farquaharson; Tenth Tennessee, Col. Randall McGavock; Third Tennessee, Col. Walker; Thirtieth Tennessee, Col. Turner; Fiftieth Tennessee, Col. Beaumont; First Tennessee Battalion, Col. Colm; Seventh Texas, Col. Granberry.

After resting awhile they renewed their march, headed by a band of music playing "The Girl I Left behind Me." They passed through Jackson amid the cheers and welcome of the people. Reaching Raymond, Miss., May 12, Gen. Gregg formed his men in line of battle, expecting an attack. Suddenly the sound of the rifle was lost amid the roar of artillery, a Confederate battery thundering away in defiance with three pieces at a six-gun battery of the Federals. At this time the force of the Federals was discovered: Gen. Gregg's Brigade was confronted by Gen. McPherson's Corps. From right to left for a mile the battle opened. Col. Randall McGavock, supported by Col. Walker, advanced with his regiment, leading in person, to charge a battery. While in the act of capturing a gun, the gallant colonel fell, mortally wounded. His tall, commanding form, clad in his gray military cloak, thrown back over his shoulders, displaying the scarlet lining, made him a very conspicuous figure at the head of his regiment.

The Tenth Tennessee seemed to be desperate after the loss of their beloved commander. All around the battery the scene is described as bloody in the extreme. Capt. George Diggon and Capt. O'Bryan were wounded. In ten minutes one hundred and ninety out of five hundred of the Tenth Tennessee were killed. The loss of the Federals was fearful in this hand to hand struggle. It was a real fight between brave men, the blue and the gray. Two thousand of Gen. Gregg's men of the "Lone Star State" kept at bay the advance of Gen. Grant's army. Gen. Gregg retreated to Mississippi Springs. As they passed through Raymond every kindness was given them. The women with their own hands brought quilts and bandages for the wounded.

Loss of Vicksburg.

It now becomes necessary to turn our narrative to the progress of events on the Mississippi river. Beginning on May 1, the Federals had successively defeated the Confederates at Port Gibson, Bayou Pierre, captured Jackson, the capital of the State of Mississippi, and driven the Confederates back at Baker's Creek and Big Black Bridge, and by the 18th had succeeded in investing Vicksburg. On May 21 Gen. Grant made a general attack upon the Confederate fortifications, but was repulsed with great loss. He then settled down for a long siege, which was continued until July 4, when the whole country was distressed that Vicksburg had surrendered, throwing into the hands of the Federals twenty thousand prisoners. The causes leading to giving up this, the key to the whole lower Mississippi region, have been much

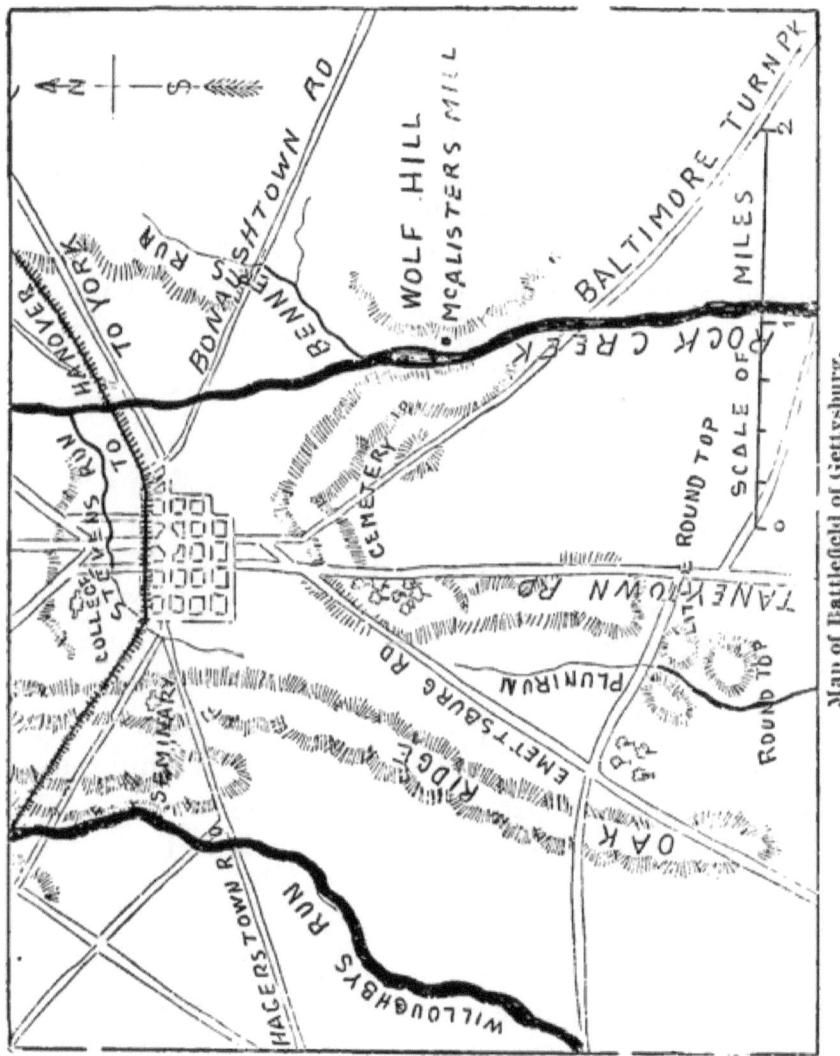

Map of Battlefield of Gettysburg.

discussed in the long years of the past; but it will be sufficient here to say that the garrison were worn out and exhausted, and Gen. Robertson, learning that the Federals were contemplating a general assault, rather than expose his weakened men, who had never failed to do their duty, to the horrors of a slaughter that must necessarily follow the siege of the city, turned the city over to Gen. Grant.

Invasion of Pennsylvania.

In our narrative we find that we are again in Virginia. Gen. Ewell had followed up the success at Chancellorsville by falling upon Gen. Milroy at Winchester and Martinsburg, Va. From this position Gen. Ewell moved rapidly up the Potomac river, followed by Gens. Longstreet and Hill. These movements threw the North in great commotion, fearing the Confederates might make an attack on Washington. Gen. Lee contented himself with the invasion of Pennsylvania. Not a stone would he have injured in the dear old edifice, the Capitol at Washington. In keeping with the magnanimity of his great heart, he protected the lives and property of the citizens of Pennsylvania, where he might have retaliated for burned homes, done by millitary orders.

Battle of Gettysburg.

We now bring before our readers the memorable battle of Gettysburg, which began July 1. Gen. Meade commanding the Federals. His advance consisted of the Eleventh Corps. Heth's Division, with Archer's Tennesseeans in advance, met them within one mile of the town of Gettysburg, and forced them back in terrible confusion. Gen. Archer was taken prisoner, with several hundred of his brigade. Gen. Ewell swept through Gettysburg, taking five thousand prisoners.

Gen. Meade massed his entire army on Cemetery Ridge. This ridge is opposite the town, extending in a westerly and southerly direction, getting less until it comes to a height called Round Top Hill, running east and west. The Confederates occupied an exterior ridge not quite so high; distance from the Federal lines, one mile and a half. Here was arranged the Confederate line of battle, Ewell's Corps on the left, beginning with Rodes's Division; on the right was the left of Hill's Corps. The right of Anderson's Division was Longstreet's left. McLaw and Hood were on the extreme right of the Confederate line, which was opposite the Federal left.

Gen. Lee here states why he compelled to give battle: "I had not intended to fight a general battle at such distance from our base unless attacked by the other side; but, finding myself unexpectedly confronted, it became a matter of difficulty to withdraw through the mountains with our large trains. At the same time the country was unfavorable for collecting supplies while in the very presence of the Federals' main body, as they were enabled to restrain our foraging parties by holding the mountain passes with troops. A battle then became unavoidable. In view of the defeat of Gen. Meade, it was thought best to renew the attack."

On July 2 Gen. Robert E. Lee scanned the height which looked upon him through frowning brows of brass and iron. He then determined to attack.

Gen. Longstreet formed against the Federals' left; Gen. Ewell dashed forward against the Federals' right, his guns keeping a continuous fire sweeping the slopes of Cemetery Hill. Gen. Anderson was ordered to support Gen. Longstreet; Heth, Pender, Pettigrew, and Archer to act as reserves. The brave general placed himself at the head of Hood's and McLaw's Divisions. Gen. Sickles' Corps, with a terrific loss, had to retreat. These two divisions of of the boys who wore the gray, whose echo reverberated through the hills, charged the steep ascent. The fire was fearful and incessant. Three hundred pieces of artillery belched forth death and destruction on every side. For two hours the battle raged for the contested point, Round Top Hill. Gen. Meade receiving immense reënforcements. Gen. Longstreet failed to drive the boys in blue from Round Top Hill. On the left, Gen. Ewell assaulted Cemetery Hill; Johnson's Division fought their way across Rocky Creek, receiving heavy loss from the fire from higher ground. Pickett's Division now reached the field of Gettysburg. Virginia soldiers! they have borne the brunt of battle, and have exhibited courage sublime.

Gen. Lee now determined to place his artillery in front of Gen. Hill's Corps. To this end, more than one hundred pieces were placed in position. On the other side of the valley Gen. Meade concentrated, preparing for the deadly conflict which was pending.

At noon, July 3, the sound of two guns fired by the famous Washington Artillery, of New Orleans, penetrated the air; in an instant two hundred cannon belched forth their contents. A Confederate officer describes the scene as follows: "The air was hideous with discordant sounds. The earth shook beneath our feet, and the hills and rocks seem to reel like a drunken man. For one hour and a half this terrific fire continued, during which time the shrieking of shells, the crash of falling timbers, the fragments of rocks flying through the air shattered from the cliffs by the solid shot, the heavy mutterings from the valley between the two armies, the blue and the gray, the bursting of shells, and the fierce neighing of artillery horses made a picture terribly grand and sublime."

Onward they moved; Pickett's Division on the right and Heth on the left of the assaulting column, Archer's Tennesseeans and Armstead's Virginians forming the center, Wilcox on the right of the Virginians. As the advance reached Emmetsburg Road, there stood those heroic soldiers exposed to the uninterrupted fire of the Federal batteries, which was so rapid and continuous that it seemed like one solid, unbroken sheet of flame that was scorching to the earth line after line, like the grass on the Western prairies; but they faltered not. Archer's Brigade of Tennesseeans was first with these Virginians to plant the battle flag on the Federal fortifications. Col. Frye, in command of Archer's Brigade, was borne away wounded, Col. Sheppard succeeding him. Night now closed in on this third day field of slaughter.

Out of twenty-four regimental officers of Pickett's Division, only two escaped unhurt; out of about the same number in Heth's Division, only one escaped. Gen. Meade states his loss at 23,000 killed, wounded, and missing; Confederates, 8,000.

For the final charge on the third day Heth's and

Pickett's Divisions were selected. Gen. Heth having been wounded on the first day, Pickett was placed in command of the assaulting column, which gave rise to this being called "Pickett's charge."

On July 4 these armies still confronted each other, each side being unwilling to renew the attack. Gen. Meade being too badly crippled to renew it, Gen. Lee crossed his army over the Potomac, and established it on the Rapidan.

CHAPTER XVI.

SIEGE OF CHARLESTON—MORGAN'S RAID.

Not satisfied with the repulse or their fleet from Charleston April 7, the Federals, under Gen. Gilmore, now determined upon vigorous operations by placing the city in a state of siege. Immediately after their reverse the Federals in large force occupied Folly Island. Not anticipating the movements of the Federals which were to follow, so many troops had been drawn from Gen. Beauregard, against his protest, to strengthen other positions, that he was left with a force inadequate for the defense and maintenance of all his batteries in the harbor.

Having finished on August 10 the erection of their fort, the Federals opened with their batteries upon Fort Morris, and sent a detachment on foot to attack Fort Wagner. This latter expedition came to grief, for when the fire of the heavy guns was turned upon them they retreated in great confusion, with a considerable loss of life. This reverse did not thwart the plans of the Federals, for, gaining a foothold on Morris Island, they constructed a battery at a distance of one and a half miles from Fort Wagner. From this position and the one on Black Island, together with their fleet of monitors and gunboats, at the dawn of day, August 18, they turned the thunders of their guns upon the Confederate fort. All day the bombardment was kept up, old Fort Sumter and Battery Gregg, at Cummings Point, contributing their share of the awful din of the cannonading. But when the shadows of evening began to fall the Federals moved an infantry column, preceded by a negro regiment, to attack the fort. With a destructive fire thinning their ranks, they pushed their way with signal gallantry to the walls of old Fort Sumter, and began to clamber over the breastworks. Here a desperate and bloody hand to hand encounter took place. As fast as the Confederates would beat back the Federals another fresh line would take their place. But finally, after lining the parapet walls with their dead, these boys in blue were compelled to give way and make a full retreat across the beach in utter darkness of the night. However the Federals were not yet prepared to give up the fort without another struggle. Consequently in less than half an hour the defenders of the fort found themselves again battling with a fresh column of the Federals, but they were repulsed even more disastrously than those who participated in the first attack, for they left behind them between two and three hundred prisoners. In both of these attacks the Federals gave their mortality at fifteen hundred and fifty, while the Confederates only suffered to the extent of a little over one hundred in killed and wounded.

On August 21 Gen. Gilmore informed Gen. Beauregard that unless Fort Sumter and Morris Island were evacuated within four hours he would turn his guns upon the city of Charleston. Without giving time for the necessary reply Gen. Gilmore sent his missiles of death into the midst of the defenseless city. For three days (August 21, 22, and 23) the Federals kept up a continuous fire upon the walls of Fort Sumter, doing great damage. On the 5th of September they turned their attention to Fort Moultrie and Battery Gregg. Upon the latter they made an especially vigorous attack by trying to get in the rear of the fortifications, but were repulsed by the effective fire from the fort, and were forced to give up their attempt. Both Morris Island and Battery Gregg had suffered so much from this continuous bombardment of over fifty days that, perceiving they were no longer tenable, on the night of September 6 Gen. Beauregard accomplished a successful evacuation, leaving these two positions, which had been so long coveted, in the hands of the Federals.

Two days later Admiral Dahlgreen, the commander of the Federal fleet, sent a demand to Gen. Beauregard for the immediate surrender of Fort Sumter, to which the reply was given that they could have it when they took it. With this, at one o'clock on the morning of September 9 the Federals began to assail the walls of the old fort that had so long stood between them and their much longed for prize. The Charleston Battalion, under Maj. Elliott, were watching and waiting, and they reserved their fire until the Federals closed upon them, when they opened fire with such volleys that this ruin (as the Federal commander reported to the government at Washington) seemed fairly vocal with the thunder of weapons, that meant death to those who wore the blue. However, they managed to land, and for half an hour engaged the Confederates in a hand to hand contest, when they were forced to surrender. The Federal reserve line, which had been left in the boat, pulled off and escaped, though followed by the shells that Fort Moultrie sent whistling after them. With not the loss of a single life, the Confederates found in their possession, as the fruits of the conflict, one hundred and twenty men, including twelve officers, with five stands of colors.

GEN. MORGAN'S RAID.

Leaving for a time the city of Charleston to the fruitless attacks of the Federals, on the other side of the mountains Gen. John Morgan was preparing to set out from Sparta, Tenn., with only two thousand troops, for that romantic raid of his into Ohio and Indiana. He began his exploits by attacking at Green River Bridge on July 4, but the fortifications were too strong. So he had to content himself with the capture of Lebanon on the next day, in which he claimed six hundred prisoners, besides many stores and arms. In this gallant charge his brother, Lieut. Thomas Morgan, fell mortally wounded with these words on his lips: "Brother Cally, they have killed me."

Thence Gen. Morgan passed through Central Kentucky to Bardstown, taking a company of cavalry dressed in blue. There is a peculiar and striking feature connected with the Confederate advance through this portion of Kentucky, in that they were in the midst of their own homes and loved ones, and were forced to carry war upon dear friends and neighbors, even father, brother, and other kinsmen who had espoused the Federal cause from conscientious motives. These divisions of family in Kentucky even marred the relation of husband and wife, for the narrator of these events knew personally of a case where the husband was a gallant soldier of the Confederacy in Gen. Frank Cheatham's Division, and his wife was an efficient and valued spy in Gen. Rousseau's command. From pure motives this woman did this work. Under such circumstances many a Kentucky mother has mourned a soldier boy whose heart's best blood stained a gray jacket at Shiloh, and another perhaps lay upon the same dread field with his body wrapped in blue for his winding sheet.

But Gen. Morgan continued his march, threatening Louisville, and crossing the Ohio river at Brandenburg. July 8 he captured the Indiana town of Corydon, with six hundred prisoners. Thence, destroying railroads, telegraph communications, and all manner of government stores, he advanced into the interior of the State, creating the greatest amount of consternation among the astonished Federals, and to the Confederates the greatest surprise.

Learning that the Federals were concentrating large numbers of troops at Indianapolis, New Albany, and Mitchell, Gen. Morgan, having accomplished his purpose by drawing troops from important places, left Indiana and entered the borders of Ohio, throwing Cincinnati into intense excitement. He proceeded to harass the Federals as he had done in the former State, until at Pomeroy he encountered a large force of Federals, several thousand strong. Leaving part of his forces to hold these in check, he attempted to cross the river at Buffington Island on July 18. Prevented from accomplishing this undertaking by Federal gunboats, he tried farther up the river at Bellville, but only succeeded in getting about two hundred of his command across the river. The latter managed to make their escape back to the Confederate lines; the remainder, who had been left on the other side of the river, fell into the hands of the Federals, among whom was the gallant Gen. John H. Morgan himself, who was captured after an exciting chase near West Point, and confined in the Ohio penitentiary until November 20, when, with six of his officers, he effected his escape by digging out with knives.

Though the end of this expedition is to be accounted a failure, yet, relatively, the two thousand prisoners which fell to the Federals were more than compensated for by the loss which this intrepid cavalryman inflicted upon them; for he had overrun two large, rich States, throwing them into a state of complete demoralization, stopping all trade, business, farming, destroying railroads, bridges, public property, steamboats, and telegraph systems, all of which in the aggregate amounted to many millions of dollars. Consequently the capture of Gen. Morgan and his men by the Federals is deprived of most of its glory in that it came too late, for the purposes of the invasion were virtually accomplished.

CHAPTER XVII.

CHICKAMAUGA—MARTIAL LAW IN KENTUCKY.

The preceding chapters in regard to military events in the West seem to furnish a striking contrast to the brilliant successes in Virginia. After the battle of Murfreesboro Gen. Bragg had fallen back to Tullahoma. Thence he proceeded to Wartrace and Shelbyville, with his army greatly weakened by the forces which had been drawn from it to strengthen the Southwest. By a flank movement, June 27, the Federals forced the Confederates to fall back to Chattanooga, Gen. Rosecrans slowly following with his grand army of boys dressed in blue, seventy thousand in number, arriving at Stevenson and Bridgeport August 20.

At the same time another movement by Gen. Burnside, with an army of twenty-five thousand, moved from Kentucky against Knoxville, Tenn., which was held by Gen. Buckner with five thousand troops. Feeling his inability to cope with such overwhelming numbers, the latter evacuated the city and moved to join Gen. Bragg at Chattanooga, leaving, however, at Cumberland Gap Gen. Frazier with two thousand troops. Against this position the Federals now turned their attention, and on the 9th of September Gen. Frazier, without firing a single gun, surrendered the garrison.

This movement was a painful surprise to the whole country, Federals and Confederates alike. It was believed that the position could have been held against the force which was being brought against it. Like many other times, mistakes were made which were unavoidable.

BATTLE OF CHICKAMAUGA.

While Gen. Burnside was pressing Gen. Buckner in front, Gen. Rosecrans had sent a corps up the Sequatchie valley to give him a blow in the rear. Gen. Buckner's command was not yet large enough to meet the Federals, so he retreated to Hiwassee. The purpose of the Federals seemed to be to threaten the Confederate rear; but the latter, though having at the very highest estimate but thirty-five thousand men, determined to offer battle at the first opportunity. Therefore on September 7 Gen. D. H. Hill moved with his corps to La Fayette, and Gen. Buckner, with the Army of East Tennessee, and Gen. Walker, with a division of the Army of Mississippi, took a position at Anderson, while Gen. Polk concentrated his forces at Lee & Gordon's Mills. Meantime the Federals' left, under Gen. Crittenden, swung around in the direction of Chattanooga, with Gen. Thomas' Corps moving toward La Fayette, and by the 9th they had crossed Lookout Mountain into McLemore's Cove. Appreciating at once the error of the Federals in allowing Thomas' Corps to become thus separated from the main army, Gen. Bragg ordered Gen. Hindman to attack the Federals, and Gen. Hill to coöperate; but the latter, believing it to be impossible to get his command through the gaps in the mountains on account of obstructions, failed to unite his forces with those of Gen. Hindman on the 10th. In great haste Gen. Buckner was ordered to fill the command which had been given to Gen. Hill, and by evening he succeeded in joining Gen. Hindman at Davis' Cross Roads; but it was too late. The Federals, perceiving their almost fatal mistake, by a series of rapid marches managed to restore their scattered divisions; and by Saturday, September 19, they held a position in the Chickamauga valley, with a creek of the same name separating them from the Confederates, who had been reënforced by two brigades from Mississippi, and five brigades from Gen. Longstreet's Corps from Virginia. The Federals opened the battle by hurling a large force upon Gen. Walker's Corps, which held a position on Gen. Buckner's extreme right. The Confederates repulsed the Federals and drove them some distance, but were themselves being forced back when they were reënforced by Gen. Frank Cheatham's Division, being held in reserve. The battle became general along the whole line. Gens. Stewart, Cleburne, and Hood in some cases had penetrated far into the Federal lines. With this auspicious beginning the Confederates gathered their energies together for a grand victory on the next day. The following was the disposition of the troops: The right wing, under Gen. Polk, consisted of Gen. Hill's Corps, composed of Cleburne's, Breckinridge's, Cheatham's, and Walker's Divisions; the left wing, under Gen. Longstreet, consisted of Gens. B. R. Johnson, Preston of Buckner's Corps, Hindman's Division, Benning's, Lane's, Robertson's, Kershaw's, and Humphries' Brigades. Breckinridge and Cleburne moved forward against the rude fortification which the Federals had erected during the night. Magnificently did these boys in gray make the attack, expecting to meet in grand array the boys in blue under command of the distinguished Maj. Gen. Thomas, who held the left, when reënforcements arrived in time for his relief. All along the line the battle waged with terrible fury, the Federals gradually giving way. Late in the afternoon the Confederates, in one solid column, swept forward with a cheer which seemed to make the mountains shake, inspired by the memories of their forced retreat from Murfreesboro before this same army of gallant soldiers who wore the blue. Like a storm cloud ready to let loose its torrents, they rushed forward. Men of Mississippi, Louisiana, South Carolina, Alabama, and Tennessee stood side by side in an unbroken, unfaltering line, and like a swollen torrent of the mountains upon which they fought with desperation forced the Federals to retreat toward Missionary Ridge. That bright September moon looked down upon the shattered wreck of Rosecrans' army. It is said that Gen. Forest had climbed a tree, and from his lofty perch watched the retreating army of Gen. Rosecrans. He shouted to a staff officer: "Tell Gen. Bragg to advance the whole army." The Federals left in the hands of the Confederates eight thousand prisoners, fifty-one pieces of artillery, fifteen thousand stands of small arms, and quantities of ammunition, with wagons, ambulances, teams, medicines, hospital stores, etc., in large quantities.

Among the dead on the Confederate side were Gens. Helm, Preston Smith, and James Deshler, and Gen. Hood was so severely wounded as to make amputation of his thigh necessary. At this great battle

Gen. Gregg was wounded, also captured, but was soon, after a desperate struggle, retaken by the Tenth Tennessee Regiment. Lieut. Col. Tom Beaumont, Maj. Chris Robertson, and Capt. Williams, of the Fiftieth Tennessee, were killed. Col. C. A. Sugg took command of the brigade through the battle, receiving several shots through his clothes. Out of one hundred and eighty-six soldiers of the Fiftieth Regiment who went into this fight, only fifty-four escaped. At the battle of Missionary Ridge Col. Sugg was ordered to charge the Federal line. This famous old regiment mounted the temporary breastworks and caused the Federals to retreat to the foot of the ridge. In this charge Col. Sugg fell mortally wounded. Capt. Sam Mays was badly wounded. Adjt. Beaumont also fell mortally wounded. September 23 Gen. Bragg moved his army from Chickamauga to Missionary Ridge, leaving the Federals in possession of Chattanooga, where they reorganized their army and fortified themselves.

Martial Law in Kentucky.

The State of Kentucky at all times seemed to have more than her share of the evils and misfortunes incident to the war, her people being equally divided between Southern and Northern sympathies. Such influences were brought to bear upon Gov. McGoffin that on August 18, 1862, he resigned his position. When the election time came round Gen. Burnside took the matter into his own hands, and declared the state under "martial law."

Orders were issued to oppress these people in many ways by the Federal government. Therefore, with such pressure as this brought to bear upon the citizens of Kentucky, the candidate who was elected (Mr. Bramlette) was virtually an appointee of the Federal government, forced into office by the strong arm of the military. Only those who have experienced that unhappy life can tell of its horrors. With such a fate as this which befell the noble State of the "dark and bloody ground" staring them in the face, one ceases to wonder at that almost superhuman endurance of the boys who wore the gray. At this time the old veteran who wore the blue ofttimes is heard to express wonder at the efforts made by those soldiers, who stood up against the vast and inexhaustible numbers which the Federals were sending here in one constant stream from every direction. The soldiers and people of the South only ended their efforts when completely worn out, like the best-tempered steel, which from long usage and the continued action of the elements, finally loses its strength and breaks.

But not only did the Confederacy have to contend with the North itself, but also indirectly with the powers of Europe; for they, especially England, made invidious distinctions between the two governments. In fact, while allowing the Federals to recruit their armies from her dominions and to get ammunition and supplies, the British government seized upon two ships which were in course of construction at Birkenhead for the Confederacy. Thus it can be seen how much the more is that struggle remarkable which the South, unaided and all alone, maintained against one of the strongest powers of modern times that marshalled its forces at her very doors.

CHAPTER XVIII.

RAPPAHANNOCK—MISSIONARY RIDGE.

At the beginning of this chapter, before taking up the thread of active operations on the land, a brief account of the navy of the Confederate States, which has heretofore been playing such an important part, would not be out of place in this narrative of important events. At the beginning of the great struggle the South was not only virtually without a fleet, but also the means of constructing one. But at once recognizing the importance of ships for coast and river defenses, she had directed her energies in this direction, and now had succeeded in floating about seventy-two vessels, twenty-nine in process of construction. This includes ships of every description with the navy since the beginning of the war. The Confederacy had succeeded in capturing over one hundred and fifty Federal ships, which, with their cargoes, aggregated a total damage of many millions of dollars.

Skirmishes on the Rappahannock.

Retreating from Pennsylvania, Gen. Lee had taken a position on the Rapidan, from which place he moved on October 9 for the purpose of meeting the Federals who were in the vicinity of Culpepper C. H., and on the 10th his right, under Gen. Stuart, met the advance line of the Federals at James City, and caused them to retreat in the direction of their main body at Culpepper C. H. On reaching the latter place, on the

11th, Gen. Lee found that the Federals had withdrawn toward the Rappahannock. However Gen. Stuart did not relax his pursuit, and continued to harass their rear. Gen. Fitzhugh Lee, who had been left to guard the Rapidan, met a detachment of Federals who had crossed the river, and drove them as far as Brandy Station, where, on the evening of the 11th, he was joined by Gen. Stuart.

With the united commands of the Confederates the Federals were forced with their cavalry to the other side of the Rappahannock. Continuing his march with the main army, Gen. Lee reached the Rappahannock at Warrenton Springs on the afternoon of the 12th. Here the Federals made a spasmodic resistance, but were soon forced to retreat by attacks of Confederate cavalry. This pursuit was kept up for three or four days, and was marked by frequent and severe skirmishes, especially at Bristoe's Station, where Gen. Hill, with two brigades, was repulsed by a superior force of Federals hid behind a railroad embankment. Besides a considerable loss in killed and wounded, Gen. Hill left in the hands of the Federals a number of prisoners. Finding that he had failed in his purpose to flank Gen. Meade, and that the latter was so near the intrenchments at Washington that it would be utterly impossible to get between him and them, Gen. Lee on the 18th again withdrew his army to the Rappahannock.

When the army first set about the movements just related Gen. Imboden had been sent down the Valley to protect Gen. Lee's left against any probable attacks of the Federals from that direction. With brilliancy and dispatch he carried out these plans, and while the main body of the army was on the retreat on the 18th he surrounded the town of Charleston, where a force of the Federals were fortified in the courthouse and jail.

To Gen. Imboden's summons to surrender, Col. Simpson, the Federal commander, replied: "Take me if you can." A few shells from the Confederate battery, however, forced the Federals from their position. The latter fled in the direction of Harper's Ferry, but were checked by the Eighteenth Cavalry and a detachment of infantry. After a short conflict the Federals surrendered themselves to the number of over four hundred. Reënforcements from Harper's Ferry now came to their support, but too late to be of service. Gen. Imboden retired before largely superior numbers, but kept possession of his spoils and prisoners.

Gen. Lee's army now held a position "on both sides of the Orange and Alexandria railroad, Gen. Ewell's Corps on the right, and Gen. Hill's on the left, with cavalry on each flank." Above the railroad bridge the Confederate general had fortified two hills on each side of the Rappahannock in order to prevent any flank movement on the part of the Federals.

In the meantime the Federals continued to rebuild the railroad which the Confederates had destroyed, and by the 6th it was discovered that they were approaching the river, with the intention of fighting their way across. They fell upon Gen. Rodes with the Second and Thirtieth North Carolina Regiments, stationed at Kelley's Ford, and drove the latter regiment to some building near the river, where they captured them.

The Federals were also directing their attention to the Confederate rifle pits at the bridge on the north bank, which were occupied by Col. Godwin, with one brigade, and Gen. Hayes, also with one brigade. Anticipating an attack, the artillery was moved to the front, and Gen. A. P. Hill's Corps, with Anderson's and Early's Divisions, were kept "watching and waiting." The Federals, however, had planned a surprise, and under the cover of darkness they hurled their overwhelming numbers against the troops stationed on the north bank of the river. In a triple line they made their attack. Their first column melted away before the destructive fire of the Confederates, but had every bullet that sped from that little band defending the pits found a lodgment in a human breast, they could not even then have maintained themselves against such a force of numbers, that by their very weight pushed them from their position and surrounded them on all sides. They fought with a courage that comes of desperation. Many were captured, and a few cut their way through the almost solid lines which surrounded them, swam the river, and made their escape. This reverse caused them to withdraw their forces to the south side of the Rapidan, where, on the 27th day of November, that portion of Gen. Lee's army drawn up at Germania Ford was attacked by a large force of the Federals, who again attempted a surprise; but they did not meet with that success which had crowned their efforts in the former attack on the Rappahannock, for they were forced to retreat with great loss, perhaps double that of the Confederates, which was four hundred and fifty in killed and wounded. This repulse seemed to put an end to Gen. Meade's designs of engaging Gen. Lee in a decisive battle.

Missionary Ridge.

The defeat at Chickamauga cost Gen. Rosecrans his command, for on October 18 he was superseded by Gen. U. S. Grant, one of the most gallant and beloved generals in the Federal army. He proceeded to Chattanooga, where the Federal forces were practically invested by Gen. Bragg. Moreover, the Confederate cavalry were keeping the Federals in a continued state of worry by their continuous and constant raids---especially that of the gallant Gen. Wheeler, in which he captured a large number of prisoners, destroyed many bridges, and took a large amount of stores of all kinds. It is our Gen. Joe Wheeler, the same who fought for the "Southern rights," that is now at this time serving our united country.

On reaching Chattanooga Gen. Grant put new life into the dispirited boys who wore the blue. On October 28 he dispatched Gen. Hooker into the Lookout valley with the Eleventh Corps and one division of the Twelfth Corps. He also succeeded in getting possession of the range of hills at the entrance to this valley. The Confederates, however, did not permit these movements to proceed in peace, for on the night of the 29th six regiments fell upon the Federals, but, after a gallant fight, they were forced to retreat, as the entire Twelfth Corps, under Gen. Slocum, were engaged against them.

In the early part of November Gen. Bragg sent Gen. Longstreet with his forces to attack Gen. Burnside at Knoxville. Upon hearing of this movement

Gen. Grant determined to attack the Confederates in their much weakened condition. Gen. Bragg had taken a position on the top of Missionary Ridge, which was between four and six hundred feet in height, and had posted his troops "along the crest of the ridge from McFarland's Gap almost to the mouth of the Chickamauga, a distance of six miles or more." Reënforced by Gen. Sherman, the Federals consumed the 23d and 24th in getting their forces in position for a general attack, and on the 25th, with a magnificent army of eighty-five thousand, Gen. Grant moved against the Confederates, who numbered one-half of that strength. At ten o'clock the Federals hurled their heavy columns, supported by large reserves, against the left, under Gen. Hardee, which consisted of Gens. Cleburne's, Walker's (commanded by Gen. Gist), Cheatham's, and Stevenson's Divisions. As became the veterans of Shiloh and Chickamauga, did these tried divisions maintain themselves against two successive assaults of the Federals, firmly holding their positions. But the left, under Gen. Breckinridge, did not fare so well when the Federals fell upon them at twelve o'clock. Somehow a brigade in the center gave way, by that means giving the Federals a foothold upon the crest of the ridge and to turn their fire upon the flanks. Soon the whole left broke and retreated, and the day was lost and the victory at Chickamauga rendered fruitless, save to give an exhibition of the courage of both armies. Though Gen. Hardee had been victorious in his encounter with the Federals, the complete disaster on the left made his success vain and fruitless. So the night of the 25th found Gen. Bragg in retreat in the direction of Dalton, Ga., with Gen. Cleburne's Division guarding the rear.

The latter's remarkably skillful, brave, and successful performance of this duty cast a brilliancy over an otherwise gloomy and disastrous movement. To make their victory more complete, the Federals sent a picked division of ten thousand men in pursuit, which the Confederates managed to repulse at every point. Especially at Taylor's Ridge did Gen. Thomas' advance came to grief.

Here Gen. Cleburne concealed his artillery and planted his infantry on both sides of the road, and when the Federals came very close upon them, with both heavy guns and muskets the Confederates turned loose such a fire that it is said "they were fairly cut to pieces," which caused them to break and flee in confusion, leaving scattered upon the bloody road fifteen hundred killed and wounded as an evidence that they had entered literally into the very jaws of death. Moreover, the brave and gallant Cleburne had in his possession two hundred and fifty prisoners, and three battle flags of the Federals; and the latter showed their appreciation of this sanguinary lesson by ceasing at once from any further pursuit.

Gen. Longstreet had been sent against Knoxville with hardly eleven thousand men, and with but an insufficient amount of supplies and means of transportation for even these. However, this did not daunt the hero of many Virginia battles; but, by taking large amounts of booty at Lenoir and Bean's Stations and in the Clinch valley, he succeeded in forcing the Federals to assist him in the maintenance of his soldier boys who wore the gray. November 18 he had forced the advance lines of the Federals into the shelter of their works, and thus had Knoxville completely invested, with every probability of an early surrender, when the news of the defeat at Missionary Ridge made it necessary for him to make an immediate assault or to retreat. The former course was decided upon. At the break of day on November 29 three brigades of McLaw's Division moved against that part of the Federal works known as Fort Sanders. Over a ground obstructed with stumps and wire ingeniously prepared by the Federals to throw the assaulting column into confusion, those gallant boys who wore the gray moved in the midst of a hailstorm of death, which placed in mourning many a once happy home in Mississippi, Georgia, and South Carolina, from which those noble boys who made up this division were drawn. However, with their comrades falling around them like the leaves of the forest when swept by an autumn gale, they pressed upon the fortifications and planted their own banner side by side with the star-spangled banner. But unavailing was this superb and unsurpassed courage, and, leaving their dead and wounded to the number of one thousand, they fell back. Gen. Longstreet took up his line of march in the direction of Rogersville, with the Federals following as far as Bean's Station, where the Confederates halted long enough to force them to retreat twelve miles, and reminding them that the veterans of Fredericksburg and Manassas were still ready to fight. Gen. Longstreet then proceeded up the State to overrun all the extreme Northeast, maintaining his entire army upon the spoils of the country.

CHAPTER XIX.

MINOR OPERATIONS IN THE WEST.

Though the operations in the extreme Southwest were on a small scale when compared with the scenes that were beng enacted on the great theater of war in the East, yet the record of how the soldiers fought—the story of the struggle for four long years of the Southern soldier against such overwhelming numbers—would be strangely lacking should one in writing a narrative omit to weave into the chronicle of events how, on September 8, the little garrison at Sabine Pass, between Louisiana and Texas, won the victory. This fort, though only mounting three guns, was attacked by a fleet of five gunboats. They disabled one of the gunboats and forced two others to surrender. Thus, with not the loss of a single man, they had gained a victory the fruits of which were, besides the two boats, two hundred men and fifteen cannons.

Many volumes might be written of those irregular bands that swept up and down the whole Western country, too few in number to risk a general battle or an open encounter with superior numbers.

About all of their actions, manner of life, their hairbreadth escapes, their heroic refusal to bow to the iron heel of oppression, preferring the long ride, the midnight surprise, choosing to be houseless and homeless wanderers, and outcasts from the lands they loved, hunted like the beasts of the forest, as mercilessly slain when found, there is the atmosphere of romantic fiction, rather than the sober, uncolored record of history. Therefore one will have to be contented with the passing tribute to their devotion to the cause they loved, with relating only one characteristic incident which took place near Fort Smith, Ark. While Quantrell and his band of "guerrillas" were in the neighborhood of the fort, Gen. Blount, accompanied by two hundred cavalrymen, rode out to meet them, thinking that they were Federal soldiers. Too late did they discover their fatal mistake. With the fierce swoop of an eagle these defenders of individual rights, as they believed, and in the rights of separate States in the far West, soon had swept the entire command from the face of the earth.

VIRGINIA AND TENNESSEE BORDER.

Near the dividing line between East Tennessee and Virginia the Confederates, under Gen. Jones, and the Federals, under Gen. Averill, were battling for supremacy in that region. On August 26 these two commands met near Dublin, and the first day's fight ended without either gaining any decided advantage. However, the Federals renewed the contest on the next day, but after two unsuccessful attacks they were forced to retreat toward Warm Springs, with the Confederates following. The latter lost between two and three hundred in killed and wounded, but took one hundred and fifty prisoners and one piece of artillery. On the 6th of the following month the Confederates gained a still more decisive victory by surprising the Federals near Rogersville, and taking (besides wagons, artillery, and cattle) eight hundred and fifty prisoners. While Gen. Ransom was per forming this brilliant achievement the Federals, seven thousand strong, were surrounding Col. W. L. Jackson at Droop Mountain, who had under his command only fifteen hundred men. But even with this small number he kept the Federals at bay for seven hours, marked by a stubborn and heroic resistance, when he was forced to retreat in the direction of Lewisburg, which retreat he successfully accomplished without the loss of either his stores or artillery. The Federal general then made a rapid raid into Virginia, destroying many supplies, especially at Salem. On his return, however, he was met near Covington by Col. Jackson, who succeeded in capturing two hundred of his command, though Gen. Averill himself managed to escape.

President Lincoln's Peace Proclamation.

About this time President Lincoln issued what is known as the "Peace Proclamation," only a few features of which we will give to show how humiliating it would have been for the South had it been accepted:

Whereas in and by the Constitution of the United States it is provided that the President shall have power to give reprieves and pardons for offenses against the United States, except in cases of impeachment; and whereas a rebellion exists, whereby the loyal state governments of several States have for a long time been subverted, and many persons have committed and are guilty of treason against the government of the United States, etc.

In this document the complete independence of the slaves was further guaranteed, and the following exceptions from its provisions were made:

All who are or shall have been civil or diplomatic officers

or agents of the so-called Confederate government; all who have left judicial stations under the United States to aid in the rebellion; all who are or shall have been naval or military officers of the said so-called Confederate government above the rank of colonel in the army or of lieutenant in the navy; also all who left seats in the United States Congress to aid in the rebellion, etc.

Such were the general characteristics of this remarkable document. One need not read far to see that it was a very peculiar "peace." One feels that the generous glow of an earnest, magnanimous desire for a cessation of hostilities which had caused the crimson tide of human life to flow out upon many a bloody field was so far wanting that one would not be wrong in designating it as a "Proclamation of Humiliation." It was like acid to a bleeding wound. It meant a confession of treason, of offense against civil and moral law. Its acceptance would have been at that time like one taking a burning brand and stamping upon his own forehead an ineffaceable acknowledgment of a crime which he had not committed. Moreover, the boys who wore the gray and had followed their commanders through those trying scenes of war were hardly willing to give them over to the uncertain fate threatened in President Lincoln's proclamation.

Under such circumstances as these, and upon such terms, the South never for a moment considered the question of peace; therefore, with the heroic purpose to die for the principles they had espoused, with a steadfast resolve not to willingly submit to a settlement which would place upon them chains of everlasting disgrace, these people resumed the third year of their struggle with an army so numerous that it would seem like the mythical warriors in the the Valley of the Walhalla, who fought all day, slaying and being slain; but who, being restored to life and strength during the night by some magical power, resumed their endless battles the next morning.

The year 1864 was opened in Virginia with Gen. Early's proposed attack upon the Federals fortified strongly at Petersburg in the latter part of January. Gen. Rosser, with his brigade, was sent on ahead of the main body, and near Petersburg he found a wagon train (ninety-six in number) loaded with a vast quantity of important stores of every description. This prize was too valuable to let slip without a struggle; so the Confederates made a charge, when the Federals retreated, leaving their wagons, which were full of needed supplies. Thence Gen. Rosser left for Petersburg, with the intention of assisting Gen. Early in the attack which they had planned upon that city. The Federals, though well fortified, did not feel willing to risk an encounter with the Confederates, abandoned the city, and, aided by the darkness, they escaped. This expedition was quite profitable. Gen. Rosser captured nearly three hundred prisoners and one thousand head of cattle.

Attack upon New Berne, N. C.

Immediately following these exploits of the Confederates in the Valley was Gen. Pickett's expedition against the Federals at New Berne, N. C., which resulted hardly less brilliantly than the former. With only two brigades, he charged the Federal outposts on Bachelor's Creek, in the vicinity of New Berne. With an impetuous rush he forced the Federals to retreat to the shelter of their fortifications. During the night a small detachment surprised and captured one of the finest gunboats of the Federals, moored in the Neuse river. After a hand to hand combat the crew was forced to surrender, but the Confederates were unable to hold the vessel on account of the fire from the batteries on the banks; therefore, rather than allow her to fall back into the hands of the Federals, they gave her over to the flames, and she was soon burned to the water's edge. The result of this enterprise was three hundred prisoners with their arms, two fine cannons, quite a goodly supply of provisions, clothing, camp supplies, a number of horses and cattle.

This series of small victories was continued in another quarter on the 10th and 11th of February. The Federals made an attack on the Confederates on John's Island, near Charleston, S. C. Being somewhat successful on the 10th, they renewed their efforts on the following day; but, the Confederates having been reënforced, they were forced to retreat hurriedly.

Battle of Ocean Pond.

The month of February was rendered still more conspicuous by a victory farther south in the pine woods of Florida. Gen. Finnegan, the Confederate commander, had with him a force too small to cope with the Federals, fully eight thousand in number, who had come under Gen. Seymour from Charleston harbor; therefore the former was forced to retreat before the Federals until he was reënforced by Gen. Colquitt, with his command, which was increased to five thousand, taking his position near Ocean Pond, awaiting the Federals. On the afternoon of the 20th the latter made their expected attack, which was but a repetition of the results which followed whenever those boys who wore the blue and the gray met in equal numbers. The Federals sustained themselves for a time, but when the boys in gray made their furious onslaught, so peculiar to them in all their battles from the Potomac to the Rio Grande, the Federals retreated in the direction of Jacksonville. They left on the battlefield three hundred dead and wounded. The Confederates had eighty killed and six hundred wounded.

CHAPTER XX.

INVASION OF MISSISSIPPI AND ALABAMA.

Gen. Grant now conceived the idea of carrying the war more thoroughly into the interior of the extreme Southern States, thus destroying the great source of Confederate supplies. This plan was put into active operation February 1, 1864, by Gen. Sherman marching out of Vicksburg with a column thirty-five thousand strong, and Gens. Grierson and Smith proceeding through the northern part of the State of Mississippi at the head of ten thousand cavalry and mounted infantry. The objective point of both of these expeditions was the city of Mobile, which place was at the same time anticipating an attack from the water by Federal gunboats. Gen. Polk was in command of the Confederate interests in this quarter, with a force not at all adequate to contend with the large Federal force. However, sending Gen. Forrest to watch the course of Gens. Grierson and Smith, he succeeded in holding Gen. Sherman in check long enough to save his supplies, also to evacuate Meridian, Miss., in good order, and retreat safely to Demopolis, Ala.

In contending with the other column Gen. Forrest added new laurels to his fame as a cavalry leader. With only a force of less than twenty-five hundred men it was necessary for him to crush this magnificently equipped cavalry of the Federals, nearly thrice his own in number. Near West Point this undaunted

Tennessecan made a stand, and, having posted his men irregularly in the bushes, he awaited the rush and onslaught of the Federals. As these brave boys in blue rode to the attack Confederate rifles began to crack, and with these whiplike reports the Federals were seen to fall in such alarming rapidity as to produce confusion and to check their advance. The empty saddles still continued to increase to such an extent as to spread a contagious terror in the ranks, and they gave up the contest and retreated.

Again, at Okolona, February 21, the Federals made a disastrous attempt to crush Gen. Forrest's small force. In this conflict the rout of the Federals was more complete than in the first, and they retreated toward Memphis.

These brilliant successes on the part of the Confederates prevented Gen. Sherman from reaping any of the fruits of his invasion of the State. Therefore he was forced to withdraw to Vicksburg his heavy column, his magnificent army, with which he expected to accomplish so much, with very barren laurels resting upon its banners. On February 25 the Federals followed this expedition by an attempt on the part of Gen. Thomas to push through the Confederate lines upon Atlanta. But this movement was checked, and the Federals were forced to fall back to Chattanooga.

LEGAL ENACTMENTS.

Besides this auspicious beginning in the field, the year 1864 was characterized by the enforcement of a few important acts of legislation: first, the funding of the currency; second, the stopping of further issues of paper money; third, a provision for greater revenues by an increase in taxation; and fourth, the sale of six per cent bonds to the amount of $500,000,-000. In addition to these financial measures the "Conscript Law" was revised and more rigorously enforced, thus placing the army on a better basis.

Federal Cavalry Raids.

In Virginia operations were continued by a plan of the Federals, with a picked body of men, to surprise and take the city of Richmond. To consummate this design, on February 28 there were three expeditions, under command of Gens. Kilpatrick and Custer and Col. Ulric Dahlgreen, respectively, having Richmond for their objective point. First, Gen. Custer collided with a detachment of Stuart's Horse Artillery, under Maj. Beckham, near Rio Mills, the Federals retreating across Rivanna River. Gen. Kilpatrick managed to get in sight of the spires of Richmond. Col. Dahlgreen fared worse than the other two; for, on his way to Richmond, he was confronted by a local battery and a force of clerks and schoolboys, whose first fire scattered Col. Dahlgreen's command in confusion, with a loss of fifty in killed and wounded. He retreated, harassed by irregular bands of Confederates, until near Walkerton, where he was attacked by Lieut. Pollard with a company of rangers, together with a few cavalry under Capt. Cox. Col. Dahlgreen was killed and part of his band captured. Papers found on the body of Col. Dahlgreen showed how well laid his plans were.

Federal Expeditions from New Orleans and Vicksburg.

Transferring our narrative of operations to the

Southwest, we find the Federals engaged in the preparation of an extensive movement in that quarter, which had for its purpose the complete subjugation of the country west of the Mississippi river. Accordingly, two large forces (one from New Orleans, under Gen. Franklin; the other from Vicksburg, under Gen. A. J. Smith) moved westward. The latter proceeded up Red River, and on the 14th captured Fort De Russy, with nearly three hundred prisoners. Thence they advanced up through that rich cotton section, destroying and confiscating many thousands of dollars' worth of this valuable commodity, and on the 16th took possession of Alexandria, La.

All three of the Federal divisions now turned their attention to Shreveport, La., as the most important point in the Southwest region. April 8, near the town of Mansfield, Gen. Banks was confronted by the Confederates under Gen. Kirby Smith. The contest raged for several hours; but, being unable to sustain themselves against the furious attacks of the boys in gray, the boys in blue began to retreat, and so continued until reënforced by Gen. Franklin. This battle cost the Federals, in killed, wounded, and missing, fifteen hundred men, eighteen cannons, and wagon trains containing a large amount of supplies.

Gen. Banks reorganized his forces, and, having been reënforced by Gen. A. J. Smith with his division, he awaited the oncoming Confederates in an open field, in which was a small hill that gave it the name of "Pleasant Hill Battle." The engagement was begun by a magnificent charge of the Confederates in a triple line. After pushing the Federals back and capturing one battery, Gen. Kirby Smith withdrew his forces to their original position and awaited further developments from the Federals; but they had suffered too much—two thousand in killed and wounded—to try the results of another conflict, and therefore retreated to Grand Ecore without having accomplished the great purpose of their expedition. Moreover, the gallant Gen. Kirby Smith had in his possession, as the spoils of war, over one thousand wagons, thirty-five cannons, and six thousand prisoners. Gen. Banks succeeded in getting his shattered army behind the guns of New Orleans.

GEN. FORREST IN KENTUCKY.

The Confederates seemed determined to have in the West an unbroken line of victories. Gen. Forrest, with his band of tireless riders, swept through Kentucky, and on the 12th of April, after a refusal of the commander, Maj. Booth, to surrender, he stormed Fort Pillow, and in half an hour had slain five hundred of the garrison and captured the remainder, together with a large amount of stores.

This attack upon Fort Pillow the Federals have been ever willing to designate as a massacre. It is true the mortality of the Federals was fearful; yet when one considers that they failed to take down their flag, and that the Confederates found opposed to them as a part of the garrison a large number of negroes (their former slaves, whom they had reared and cared for, and who now turned to bite the hand that fed them), then one can appreciate the thorough exasperation with which they fought.

Gen. Forrest at once moved against Paducah, Ky.,

on the 25th, and forced the Federals, who were two thousand strong, to retire. He took possession, destroying vast quantities of stores.

Confederates Retake Plymouth, N. C.

Across the mountains, in the "Old North State," the Confederates were preparing to place yet another star in their brilliant constellation of victories. The Federals had strongly fortified Plymouth, on the south bank of the Roanoke river. Against this place Gen. Hoke organized an expedition, which consisted of three brigades, commanded by Gen. Ransom and Cols. Mercer and Terry, and one regiment of cavalry under Col. Dearing, with seven batteries of artillery, commanded by Maj. Reid and Col. Branch. April 17 the expedition arrived in the vicinity of the town, and turned their artillery upon Warren's Neck, about one mile above. The result of the bombardment was much damage to the fort and the destruction of one of the gunboats which had come to its help. This was followed by an attack on Fort Wessell the next day, which surrendered after a brave resistance. In this assault Col. Mercer lost his life. Next morning the Confederate ironclad Albemarle steamed past the Federal batteries and attacked two of their gunboats. One was sunk, but the other escaped. On the morning of the 28th a general attack was made. With cheers the Confederates took battery after battery. The Federals retreated, leaving all the forts, sixteen hundred prisoners, immense quantities of supplies, and twenty-five cannons.

CHAPTER XXI.

In Virginia Again.

Attention is once more turned to the grand old "Mother State," upon whose bosom is soon to take place the final struggles which are to decide the fate of the new government which has been battling so nobly, so superbly, for her independence. The Federal government had transferred Gen. Grant to the East, with the hope and expectation that he would repeat in this new field that characteristic success which had marked his career in the West, and had put under him as magnificently equipped an army as had ever stepped to the sound of martial music. Each side somehow had a premonition that this was to be the final and decisive campaign, that there was going to be a mighty struggle in which one cause or the other was going to die. The victories that the gray lines had been gaining in the South made the Southern heart throb with a new hope, into which no element of despair or doubt entered; therefore it was with buoyant and confident step that the veterans of Lee's army marched out to meet the two huge columns which Gen. Grant set in motion on the 4th of May. On the following day they had crossed the Rapidan, and were making an attempt to turn Gen. Lee's right flank, which consisted of Gen. Edward Johnson's Division, holding a position along a turnpike. The attack of the Federals was made with vigor, and for a time it seemed as if it would be successful. But their apparent good fortune was only temporary, for the break they had made in the Confederate lines was soon closed up, while at the same time Gordon's Brigade struck them a severe blow in front that sent them reeling back in confusion. The Federals made a second attack upon another part of Gen. Johnson's line—the left—but were warmly received by Pegram's and Hays's Brigades, and hurled back after the manner of their first attack. Not satisfied with these advances, the Federals made a still more determined effort against Heth's and Wilcox' Divisions, which lasted from three o'clock until dark. But they made no impression upon that unbroken line of gray, and it was confessed from their own standpoint "that no cheer of victory swelled through the wilderness that night." The next day was consumed in assaults by Gens. Hill and Longstreet upon Hancock's Corps; but, though the line of the Federals was broken in several places by the effective blows of these two tried corps, yet they managed in the main to hold their position. Toward evening, however, the Confederates succeeded in capturing a large part of Gen. Seymour's Brigade, and this action created among the Federal forces such consternation that at one time it seemed that their whole army was on the point of a panic.

On the following day (the 7th) Gen. Grant moved his army in the direction of Fredericksburg, with the intention, it seems, of taking this route to Richmond. On the 8th, at Spottsylvania C. H., Gen. Warren's Corps received two severe repulses at the hands of Gen. Longstreet's Corps, which was now under the command of Gen. Anderson, for the former had been wounded in the battle two days before. This ended matters until Thursday, the 12th, when the Federals moved against the Confederate fortifications, and before the latter could recover themselves they had surrounded and captured nearly all of Johnson's Division. It was a critical point. The fate of the Confederacy almost hung in the balance. The Federals seemed now to be on the point of a decisive victory, that would throw open the gates of Richmond. Gen. Lee rode forward in front of the lines he had so often led to conquest and success. The scene was dramatic in its subdued intensity. He took a position "opposite at the time to the colors of the Forty-Ninth Regiment of Pegram's Brigade. Not a word did he say. He simply took off his hat 'as he sat on his charger.' An eyewitness says of him: 'I never saw a man look so noble or witnessed a spectacle so impressive.' At this interesting moment Gen. Gordon, spurring his foaming charger to the front, seized the reins of Gen. Lee's horse, and, turning him around, said: 'General, these are Virginians! They have never failed! They never will; will you, boys?' Amid loud cries of 'No, no! Gen. Lee, to the rear! Go back, go back! Gen. Lee, to the rear! Gen. Gordon gave the command, 'Forward, charge!' With this the inspiration of the battle was upon them. The heroes of Jackson were again themselves, and grandly did they fight through all that terrible day in a manner fully worthy of that grim warrior under whom they had swept so gloriously up the Valley." The shadows of night dropped their dark curtain on a theater upon whose stage had been played in awful reality one of the fiercest of all the acts in the dread tragedy of this war. Ewell, Longstreet, and Hill had flung column after column of Federals back, each time piling the ground thick with dead and dying, for the outflow of the crimson tide of human life stained between eighteen and twenty-five thousand blue uniforms, and perhaps seven thousand of the gray. But the Federals also had in their possession the three thousand prisoners of Johnson's Division and the twenty pieces of artillery captured at the same time.

While Gen. Grant was thus trying to break Gen. Lee's front, Gen. Sheridan was sent to coöperate with Gen. Butler, who was to move against Richmond from the south. On his route to Turkey Island on the 10th, at Yellow Tavern, he was opposed by Gen. J. E. B. Stuart with his cavalry. In this encounter the gallant Stuart, the very soul of Virginia chivalry, laid down his life for the country for which he had done so much and at whose hands he deserves a high rank in the calendar of heroic names in remembrance of which the South has planted an evergreen of immortality.

On the 5th of May Gen. Butler advanced, with a large force and a fleet of gunboats, up the James river, and landed and proceeded to intrench himself around Drewry's Bluff; but he was forced to abandon this position when Gen. Beauregard struck him such a forcible blow on the right as to crush it, inflicting a loss of several thousand in killed, wounded, and prisoners.

There was still another feature of the enemy's extensive operations in Virginia by which they hoped to effect a speedy destruction of the Confederacy. Gen. Sigel, with twelve thousand troops, was sent up the Shenandoah against Staunton, Gen. Crook with six thousand against Dublin, and Gen. Averill with two thousand five hundred cavalry against Wytheville. The first, under Gen. Sigel, felt the might of Gen. Breckinridge's army at Newmarket when the latter punished him to the extent of a large number in killed and wounded, six cannons, and nearly one thousand stands of arms. At Dublin Gen. Crook was sent back in full retreat by Gen. McCausland with only a force of one thousand five hundred. Besides a severe loss in killed and wounded, the Federals left in the hands of the Confederates nearly seven hundred prisoners. Gen. Averill's attack upon Wytheville was no more successful, for he was repulsed by Gen. Morgan with a heavy loss. Thus it will be seen that the plans of the Federals were thoroughly and completely baffled at every point and brought to naught.

COLD HARBOR.

On the 18th the guns were again thundering along the lines holding the approaches toward Richmond, for the tenacity of the Federal commander expressed itself in another fruitless assault upon Gen. Ewell's position. Gen. Grant changed his position again and again, but each time the ever-watchful Lee threw his insuperable wall of gray between him and the devoted city. The former, however, kept testing the strength of this wall by attacks on the 23d and 25th, and at the same time continued to swing his line around until by the 28th he had his army across the Pamunky river, and by the 1st of June was near Cold Harbor, with the object for which they had struggled so long almost in sight. But the fruition of their hopes was yet to be deferred, and the successful consummation of their plans, which seemed now at hand, to be shattered like a crystal fabric of frail glass by the blow which they received at Cold Harbor. On the morning of Friday, June 3, the Federals massed their forces against the Confederates intrenched along the Chickahominy. Assault after assault was made, and each time the Federals were hurled back, the Confederates retaining every position and giving no evidence of weakness at any point of their line save in one instance on the left, which was quickly repaired. Thus the Federals were again made to feel the effectiveness of those blows that had so completely held at bay each successive "On to Richmond" expedition. The Federals paid the penalty for their attack upon the Confederate lines with ten thousand men.

It seemed now that this leader, whom the North had chosen to lead them to a decisive victory, was to fare at the hands of Gen. Lee just as his predecessors had fared, for from a Federal historian his loss so far in this campaign was sixty thousand men, while the same authority gives the Confederate loss at a little over half that number.

The Western Part of Virginia.

The Federals were not satisfied with the repulses which they had met in the western part of Virginia. Accordingly they prepared a large force and put it under command of Gen. Hunter. To oppose this force the Confederates could only bring three small divisions—neither large enough to be called an army—commanded respectively by Breckinridge, McCausland, and William E. Jones. By the 5th of June the Federals had accomplished the capture of Staunton, in defense of which the brave and eccentric Gen. Jones lost his life. Several days later Gen. Hunter united to his own command those of Gens. Cook and Averill, and moved in the direction of Lynchburg.

Attack upon Petersburg.

Gen. Grant now determined to put forth a greater effort for the capture of the city of Petersburg, which had already on the 9th of June repulsed an attack from Gen. Butler. Active preparations were begun on the 14th by Gen. Smith with his forces assaulting and getting possession of the first line of Confederate fortifications on the northeast. This was followed on the 16th by an attack of three corps of the Federal army on the front, which were not only repulsed, but the Confederates themselves became the attacking party and drove the Federals before them and captured some of their artillery, together with a large portion of an entire regiment. The next day the Federals repeated these tactics with the same results, but on the 18th they made one more effort to get possession of the city, which, as Gov. Wise said in the beginning, "is to be and shall be defended on her outer walls, on her inner lines, at her corporation bounds, in every street and around every temple of God and altar of man." Three times during the day did the Federals hurl their heavy columns against the fortifications, but all to no purpose. The Confederates still held possession, having inflicted upon their opponents a loss of ten thousand in killed and wounded.

Other Reverses of the Federals.

The Federals seemed now to be meeting with reverses all along their lines. At Port Walthall Junction Pickett's Division had struck Gilmore's command a blow that put him to flight, while Hampton's Cavalry had served Sheridan in a similar manner on June 10 at Trevillian Station, and on the 18th Hunter was sent back to the mountains, having been repulsed from his anticipated attack upon Lynchburg, with a loss of thirteen pieces of artillery. Southwest Virginia was also saved by Gen. Morgan's bold advance into Kentucky, which forced the Federals to follow him in order to protect that State.

While these offshoots, so to speak, from the main stem of Gen. Grant's purposes were being nipped in the bud, he himself was made to suffer when the Confederates under Gen. Anderson fell upon the Second and Sixth Corps, penetrated their line, and took one battery and one whole brigade. Still another Federal expedition, commanded by Wilson and Kautz, was defeated a score of miles south of Petersburg. At the hands of Gens. Hampton, Mahone, and Finnegan they lost sixteen hundred prisoners, together with artillery, wagons, stores, and small arms.

Gen. Grant now determined that he must do something to retrieve the disasters which were falling upon him thick and fast. Therefore he resorted to the method of undermining and blowing up the principal fortifications around Petersburg. The mine was constructed under Cemetery Hill, and at half past four o'clock on the morning of July 30 the match was applied, and a mighty gap was rent in the earth by the explosion. Simultaneous with this the thunders of a hundred guns were opened upon the city, which was a signal for a general attack on the part of the Federals, hoping to take the Confederates unawares, but they discovered how completely they had mistaken the latter when they found themselves driven back in rout and confusion, many falling into the crater, making with their own dead and dying the chasm which they themselves had constructed a pit of horrors. This experiment cost Gen. Grant over five thousand men, while the loss of the Confederates was comparatively light—about one thousand men.

The Loss of the Alabama.

The ardor of the Confederates, however, was somewhat chilled by the loss of their most formidable ship of war, the Alabama, under the command of Capt. Semmes. On the 19th of June, off the harbor of Cherbourg, France, Capt. Semmes offered battle to the Federal ship Kearsarge. The latter was so well protected by iron plating and chains that the shot of the Alabama made little impression upon her, while her own shot were so effective that in a short time it was discovered that the Confederate vessel was in a sinking condition, and Capt. Semmes was forced to haul down his colors.

CHAPTER XXII.

GEN. SHERMAN IN THE SOUTH.

WHILE Gen. Grant was moving against Richmond, Gen. Sherman was preparing for an invasion of the South with an army of ninety-eight thousand men divided into three great divisions, under Gens. Thomas, Schofield, and McPherson. To oppose these mighty columns Gen. Joseph E. Johnston could bring into the field an active army of not over forty thousand men.

Gen. Sherman now moved in the direction of Dalton, Ga., and met his first check on the 14th of May in the Resaca valley, when he attempted to carry the Confederate works. The Federals were driven back with a loss of two thousand men. Gen. Johnston gradually fell back before the advancing legions of the Federals, but all the time waiting and watching for an opportunity to strike a blow, if the Federals should expose any weak point or commit a blunder. By the 20th he had crossed the Etowah river, and on the 25th he encountered the fortifications of the Federals near Dallas. The latter assumed the offensive by hurling Hooker's Corps against Stewart's Division at New Hope Church; but, after struggling for two hours to drive the Confederates from their position, the Federals were repulsed. All day during the 26th and until five o'clock in the afternoon of the 27th was consumed in skirmishes between the two armies, when the Federals again essayed an assault upon the Confederates. Cleburne's brave division received their attack this time at the hands of Howard's Corps. The latter were again beaten back, with an estimated loss of perhaps three thousand men, while the Confederates only suffered to the extent of four hundred and fifty. Lieut. Gen. Polk was killed on Pine Mountain on the 14th of June.

Gen. Johnston still kept up his brilliantly conducted retreat, striking the Federals now and then some severe blows, until he reached Kennesaw Mountain, where he made a stand. The huge column of Federals made a strong attack on the 27th of June, but they were met by the veteran troops of Cheatham's and Cleburne's Division of Hardee's Corps, together with French's and Featherstone's Divisions of Loring's Corps, and the result was that they were repulsed with a frightful loss of fully three thousand men, according to their own reports. Thence Gen. Johnston was forced to withdraw to the fortifications of Atlanta, which the Federals at once besieged.

The wise and cautious Johnston was superseded by the rash, lion-hearted, but unfortunate Hood, who would not patiently endure a siege, but suddenly hurled a column, led by Walker's and Bate's Divisions of Hardee's Corps, against the Federals' right at Peach Tree Creek. Grandly they charged with that cheer which had been the sound to which they had rushed to many a glorious victory; but with marvelous rapidity the Federals managed to mass their artillery upon them, and they were forced to withdraw. Two days later, July 22, by a second attack with Hardee's Corps the Federals were driven from their fortifications, leaving in the hands of the Confederates nearly two thousand prisoners, twenty-two pieces of artillery, and five stands of colors.

This was followed by an attempt to destroy all the railroads around Atlanta. For this purpose two forces of cavalry, under Gens. Stoneman and McCook, were to meet near Lovejoy, and fall upon the Confederate cavalry under Gen. Wheeler. Both of these expeditions proved to be hardly adequate for their task; for Gen. Stoneman was encountered near Macon, and he and one thousand of his men were captured. Gen. McCook, with one thousand men, was also captured at this place.

On the 28th of July Gen. Hood made a vigorous assault upon the Fifteenth Corps, but he was repulsed with a loss of fifteen hundred men. How grandly the Confederates moved to this attack forced from Gen. Sherman this remark: "His [Hood's] advance was magnificent." For several weeks the Federals kept up an almost ceaseless bombardment upon the city, until on the 18th of August Sherman moved his line upon the road toward Macon, in order to cut off Gen. Hood's supplies. The latter then sent his cavalry, under Gen. Wheeler, to harass the Federals.

Meantime a part of the Confederates, under Gen. Hardee, had intrenched themselves at Jonesboro, a distance of twenty-two miles from that portion under Gen. Hood at Atlanta. Quickly perceiving this unfortunate position of the Confederates, Gen. Sherman threw his army between the two positions. By the 30th of August the Federals had succeeded in crossing Flint River, and had taken up a position near

Jonesboro, where they were subjected to a fruitless attack from Gen. Hardee. This was followed on the 1st of September by an assault from the Federals themselves, with a largely superior force, and the Confederates found it necessary to retreat, and allowed the Federals the possession of the prize for which they had been struggling for more than three months, but kept at bay by an army much less than half their own. To the protests coming from both Gen. Hood and the mayor of Atlanta the Federal general replied that "war is cruelty, and you cannot refine it," forgetting that modern, civilized warfare had for its arena the battlefield, where either one side or the other prevailed through superiority in courage and skill, and not the oppression of the women and children in the cities which chance or conquest might throw into its hands.

Gen. Forrest at Tishomingo Creek.

A Federal expedition, under Gen. Sturgis, had been sent out from Memphis for the purpose of following in the rear of Gen. Sherman and coöperating with him.

By a singular coincident on the 13th of June they came in contact at Guntown with the terrible Forrest and his band, who had perpetrated the so-called "massacre" at Fort Pillow. Short, sharp, and effective were the blows which this redoubtable cavalryman struck, and the result was that two thousand of Sturgis' force were taken prisoners, and almost as many were killed and wounded.

Gen. Early's Raid.

In Virginia the Confederates assumed the offensive

by Gen. Early's raid into Maryland. On the 3d of July he moved forward near Harper's Ferry, frightening Sigel so badly at Martinsburg that he retreated to Sharpsburg, leaving in the hands of the Confederates a quantity of valuable stores. After two severe engagements the Federals were again forced to fall back to Maryland Heights, where they were re-enforced by Gens. Max Weber and Lew Wallace; thence they took a position at Monacacy Bridge, four miles from Frederick City. Here intrenched they were attacked by Gen. Early, and after a contest of two hours' duration they were defeated, with a loss of over one thousand in killed and wounded and seven hundred prisoners, while the Confederates won their victory at a cost of five hundred in killed and wounded.

Thence Gen. Early advanced toward Washington, throwing the city into a state of complete consternation and terror, for his attack was hourly expected. But the Confederates contented themselves with withdrawing across the Potomac, with a vast quantity of booty as the fruits of their expedition, among which were "five thousand horses and twenty-five hundred beef cattle." However the Federals did not allow him to depart in peace, but a force fifteen thousand strong, under Gen. Crook, followed him, which Gen. Early turned upon about five miles from Winchester, and thoroughly routed, with a loss of over one thousand, while he himself hardly suffered to the extent of sixty men.

GEN. JOHN MORGAN INVADES KENTUCKY.

Coincident with Gen. Early's expedition was Gen.

Morgan's second invasion of the State of Kentucky. In rapid succession the Confederates captured Paris, Georgetown, Cynthiana, Williamstown, and Mt. Sterling. At the latter place on the 9th of June Gen. Morgan encountered Gen. Burbridge. The Federals had been in pursuit since the Confederates left Pound Gap. This engagement was barren of decisive results to either side, and Gen. Morgan continued his work of destruction, burning the Federals' cars and depots, and capturing two regiments of prisoners at the town of Cynthiana, which was also destroyed. However, while at breakfast at this place on the morning of June 12, the Confederates were surprised by the Federals under Gen. Burbridge, and, though the former had fought nobly for an hour, they were defeated, losing six hundred in killed and wounded and nearly four hundred prisoners.

General Price in Missouri.

Gen. Price's raid into Missouri in the latter part of the month of September was equally wanting in any material benefit. He attacked the Federals, who were strongly fortified at Pilot Knob, eighty-six miles south of St. Louis, and forced them to evacuate the place. The Confederates pursued the Federals as far as Rolla, and then desisted, and without further operations went into winter quarters.

The "Peace" Question.

About this time the question of peace between the two sections was again agitated. So much blood was being spilled, and so much money spent, that at the North, as was made evident from the tone of the leading newspapers, was growing a strong sentiment toward the establishment of peace on terms honorable to both sides. To show what the South had done in the effort to put a stop to a war that was drawing from the peaceful walks of life over three million men, it would be well to quote from a letter of President Davis on the subject:

> We have made three distinct efforts to communicate with the authorities at Washington, and have been invariably unsuccessful. Commissioners were sent before hostilities were begun, and the Washington government refused to receive them or hear what they had to say. A second time I sent a military officer with a communication addressed by myself to President Lincoln. The letter was received by Gen. Scott, who did not permit the officer to see Mr. Lincoln, but promised that an answer would be sent. No answer has been received. The third time, a few months ago, a gentleman was sent whose position, character, and reputation were such as to insure his reception were not the Federals determined to receive no proposals whatever from the government. Vice President Stephens made a patriotic tender of his services, in the hope of being able to promote the cause of humanity; and although little belief was entertained of his success, I cheerfully yielded to his suggestion that the experiment should be tried. They refused to let him pass through their lines or to hold any conference with them. He was stopped before he reached Fortress Monroe on his way to Washington. To attempt again (in the face of these repeated rejections of all conference with us) to send commissioners or agents to propose peace is to invite insult and contumely, and to subject ourselves to indignities without the slightest chance of being listened to.

This letter is given to show the nature of the opinion at the South. The people of this section were battling for a principle which was, in their eyes, very essential to the freedom and prosperity of Republican institutions; but, however firm and tenacious their belief in the righteousness of this principle, even in the moment of victory they ever showed themselves willing and ready to stop the ceaseless flow of blood upon a fair and equitable basis. But on the other hand, that party represented by the government at Washington, inasmuch as it had come into power with the tide of a war, showed no disposition to treat with the Southern States on any but the most humiliating terms, and would accept no proposition coming from them which looked toward an amicable and honorable settlement.

Gov. Seymour, of New York, made the following arraignment of the character of the government: "They were animated by intolerance and fanaticism, and blinded by ignorance of the spirit of our institutions, the character of our people, and the condition of our land. . . . They will not have the union restored unless upon conditions unknown to the Constitution. . . . We are shackled with no hates, no prejudices, no passions. We wish for fraternal relations with the people of the South. We demand for them what we demand for ourselves: the full recognition of the rights of the States."

CHAPTER XXIII.

BATTLE OF MOBILE BAY—GEN. GRANT IN VIRGINIA.

[Contributed by Lieut. Wharton, who was on board the Tennessee at the time.]

THE entrance to Mobile bay was defended in the summer of 1864 by Forts Gaines and Morgan, on opposite sides of the entrance, about two and a half miles apart; but as the channel was close to the latter, it was practically the defense of the harbor. A line of torpedoes extended across the channel. In addition there was a Confederate squadron of four vessels, the Morgan, Gaines, and Selma, wooden gunboats, and the ironclad Tennessee. Fort Morgan mounted eighty-six guns and the squadron twenty-two guns. All told, the Confederates had one hundred and eight guns and eleven hundred men. The Federal fleet attacking was composed of fourteen wooden vessels and four monitors, mounting two hundred guns, and manned by twenty-seven hundred men.

On August 5, 1864, the Federal fleet got under way from off the entrance and advanced to the attack, the monitors leading in a single line and the wooden vessels lashed together two and two. At 6:45 A. M. the leading monitor fired the first shot at the fort; and soon after, as the Federal fleet advanced, the firing became general between the fort and the fleet. But a fateful moment was approaching. The bow gun of the Tennessee was loaded with a rifled one

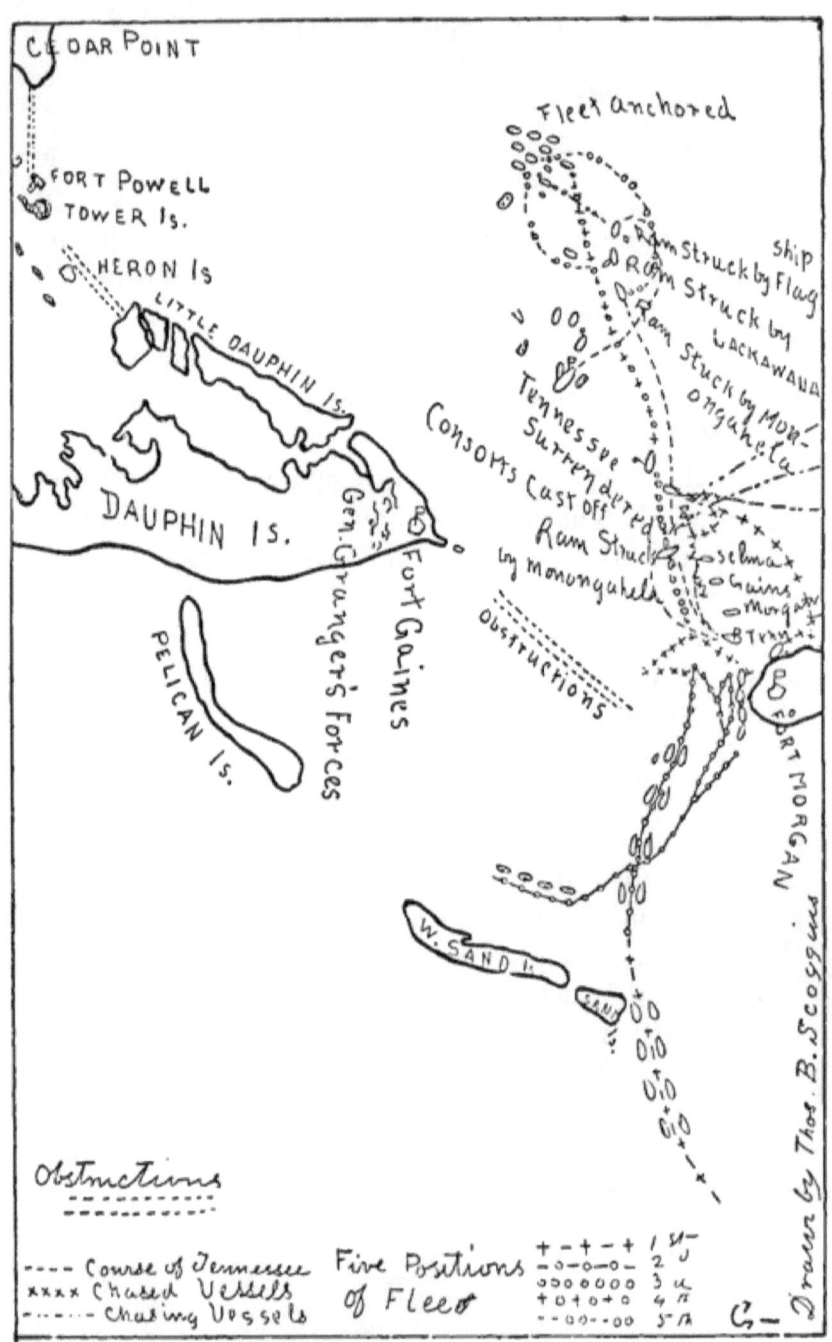

Naval Engagement in Mobile Bay.

hundred and forty pound bolt, to be fired at the first of the monitors when the two should come together. *It was never fired at her.* As the Tecumseh neared the line of torpedoes her bow was gradually seen to sink, the water rose upon a slanting turret, she was over on her side, her screw visible in air, and then she was out of sight. One hundred and thirty souls perished there in less than ten seconds. A few men only were seen to leap wildly from her turret as she went down. There was no disturbance of the water except the splash and gurgle she made in sinking. The full force of the terrible torpedo expended itself inside the vessel.

The sinking of this finest and most formidable of the Federal ships demoralized the head of the line, and they began to back. Seeing disgrace and defeat imminent if this were permitted, Admiral Farragut boldly steamed out of his place in the middle of the Federal fleet and led it, regardless of torpedoes—no more of which exploded—straight for the bay. A terrific fight ensued between the fort and Confederate squadron on one side and the Federal fleet on the other. Over two hundred guns were being fired at one time. By eight o'clock the last vessel had passed in, their loss being great in killed and wounded. On the Confederate side the Selma, an open-decked vessel most bravely fought by her captain, P. W. Murphy, had been captured, the Gaines sunk, and the Tennessee and Morgan left. The latter was of no further use in fighting so overwhelming a force.

A very few minutes after the Federal fleet had anchored in the bay, some three miles up, Admiral Buchanan ordered Capt. Johnston to take the Confederate flagship Tennessee again into action. *One* ironclad against *three* monitors and fourteen wooden men-of-war! Tremendous odds! But there was nothing else to do. A magnificent display of bravery was now made for about two hours. This solitary vessel was in the midst of her foes, firing in every direction. She was the focus of the fire of two hundred guns, and shot and shell rained upon her sides like a deluge. Five times was she rammed by swiftly moving frigates, but she only spun around after the impact and sent shot and shell hurtling home until, smokestack and steering gear gone and port shutters jammed, she lay a log upon the water. When nothing else was possible, she surrendered. The Confederate loss on the little squadron was eight killed and ten wounded; on the Federal fleet the total loss was three hundred and fifty-two.

In a day or two Fort Gaines was captured, but Gen. Page gallantly held Fort Morgan until the 23d of August, when, surrounded by fleet and army, he surrendered after a fierce bombardment of many hours. Mobile was held by the Confederates until the 8th of April, 1865.

Destruction of the Florida and Albemarle.

This naval disaster was followed by the destruction of two Confederate vessels. On the 7th of October the privateer Florida was anchored in the neutral harbor of San Salvador, in Brazil, with most of her crew upon the shore, when she was run into and captured by the Federal vessel Wachusetts. For this outrage and violation of the laws of nations the government at Washington afterwards apologized to Brazil.

On the 27th of the same month the ram Albemarle was exploded by a torpedo in the Roanoke river, but the agents in this expedition under Lieut. Cushing were captured.

THE ATTEMPTS UPON RICHMOND.

On the night of the 28th of September the Federals again resumed their efforts against the Confederate line around Richmond by crossing to the north side of the James in large force. On the next morning the Federals hurled their column against the Confederate position at the Phillips House on Four Mile Run, but had the misfortune to encounter the Texas brigade, and were repulsed with great loss. They followed this with another attack on Market Heights, with results equally disastrous. Another column of the Federals succeeded in getting possession of Fort Harrison before assistance could reach it, and then they advanced upon Fort Gilmer, but the gallant Confederates repulsed them and sent them back with great loss. This action closed the day's fighting, and it was found that the Federals had lost over four thousand in killed and wounded, with six flags and five hundred prisoners. On the next day (the 30th) Gen. Field made an unsuccessful attempt to retake Fort Harrison, but, owing to a failure of support just at the proper time, he was repulsed.

The dawn of October 6 saw the Confederates with Gen. Geary's Brigade of cavalry make a brilliant attack upon the Federals' right on the Charles City road, about five miles from Richmond. The latter were driven back to their works, but the Confederates did not stop, but in their enthusiasm they rushed over the works, pushing the Federals out, and capturing seven hundred prisoners, nine guns, and one hundred horses. The Federals made another stand at their second line of intrenchments; but they melted away before the impetuous onslaught of the Confederates, and fled to the shelter of the guns of Fort Harrison. Reënforced, they returned to retake the works from which they had been beaten; but the Confederates sent them back shattered and broken with terrible loss, and night put an end to the contest.

On the 27th Gen. Grant made an effort to turn Gen. Lee's left flank, and was advancing his columns by the Williamsburg and Nine Mile roads. The works on the latter position had been taken by three brigades of negro troops; but they could not maintain themselves long, for Hampton's Legion and the Twenty-Fourth Virginia drove them back with terrible slaughter. On the other road (the Williamsburg) the Federals had stationed their batteries, and were pouring shots and shells into the Confederate works. The latter endured this cannonading in silence, and thus misled the Federals into making a charge. Having reserved their fire until the Federals were close upon them, they made the ground tremble with the terrific thunder of their artillery and musketry, and the Federals broke and fled in confusion, with a loss, besides a considerable number in killed and wounded, of five hundred prisoners. Again, the attack upon the gray lines on the Boydton road proved no less disastrous to the Federals, for Gen. Mahone received them so valiantly that he soon had them in full retreat, leaving with the Confederates as their spoils of victory over four hundred prisoners.

Thus this human wall was still between the capital of the Confederacy and the Federals. With unbroken front the latter were met at every point, and in this autumn of 1864 they seemed as far from gaining their object as in the fall of 1861. But still the Federal general persisted, and made up in tenacity for any lack of military genius. Surely he must have had a certain premonition that one day these gray veterans who flung themselves so often between him and the goal of his struggles must inevitably succumb to the solid and almost innumerable lines which he was throwing around them, however heroically they might fight.

Sheridan's Raid in the Valley.

Coincident with his operations in the immediate vicinity of the city, the Federal commander adopted another plan, which, if successfully consummated, would deprive Gen. Lee of his source of supplies from the rich, productive valley of the Shenandoah. For this purpose Gen. Hunter was superseded on the 8th of August by Gen. Sheridan, who had under his command no less than three corps, together with the divisions of Cook, Averill, and Kelly. With this large force he proceeded to take possession of Martinsburg, Williamsport, and Winchester, Gen. Early falling gradually back before his advance. Near Winchester, however, on the 19th of September, though outnumbered nearly four to one, the Confederates made a stand. The Federals moved to the attack, and the engagement was stubbornly and hotly contested. One division of the Federals was broken and thrown into confusion, which the Confederates took advantage of and charged. A glorious victory seemed almost in their hands. The impetuous rush of Early's men was carrying everything before it, and the Federals were obliged to call their reserves to the rescue in order to restore their shattered lines. Unfortunately the Federals fell upon the Confederate cavalry on the left and threw it into confusion, which made a retreat necessary. Gen. Early then took up a strong position at Fisher's Hill, whither the Federals followed, and on the 22d moved to attack him. With their large numbers the Federals managed to literally surround Gen. Early's command and to force them from their intrenchments, driving them beyond Port Republic with a loss of over seven hundred prisoners. This victory left the Federals in complete possession of the rich valley, and they at once turned themselves loose in it, pillaging and destroying everything of worth and value, so that along their track were ruin and desolation. Farm and manufactory were leveled to the earth as if by the breath of a hurricane, and the beautiful and picturesque valley, that fairly blossomed like a garden, became as a desert and a waste place.

BATTLE OF CEDAR CREEK.

The undaunted Early, in spite of his two defeats, was not yet prepared to allow the Federals to rest on their laurels without another struggle; therefore we find him again at Fisher's Hill on the 18th of October "with two corps of Sheridan's army in his front on the north side of Cedar Creek. Another corps, the

Sixth, was between Middletown and Newtown. Sheridan himself was at Winchester, with his cavalry a little withdrawn from the front." By a toilsome, arduous night march through a mountainous country, with the Shenandoah to be crossed twice, Gen. Early placed himself in front of the Federals. With a gallant, sweeping charge, he struck terror to them, taking them completely by surprise, and soon had Sheridan's magnificent army of three corps in a confused, panic-stricken retreat, leaving in the hands of the victorious Confederates their camps with one thousand five hundred prisoners; but the fatal mistake was made of stopping to plunder the abandoned booty of the Federals. This gave them time to reorganize their demoralized divisions and to renew the battle. Misfortune followed misfortune. In one of those inexplainable moments that come to men whose courage has been tested upon a hundred battlefields, the followers of Early, that had made illustrious the army of Virginia, gave way in a disordered retreat, sustaining a total loss of three thousand, while the glory of one of the grandest victories of the war was just in their grasp. With this reverse the larger portion of his army was transferred to assist Gen. Lee around Richmond.

Gen. Breckinridge in East Tennessee.

While these important battles were taking place in Northern Virginia Gen. Breckinridge had administered two severe defeats upon the Federals in the Southwest: one on the Holston river on the 2d of October, and one at Morristown, Tenn., on the 18th of November. On the 20th of the following month the Federals made a raid into Virginia, capturing the salt works at Saltville, and, forcing the Col. Preston to evacuate Fort Breckinridge, they sacked the town of Abingdon.

BATTLE OF JOHNSONVILLE.

Gen. Forrest reported to Gen. Dick Taylor at Cherokee Station, Ala., and requested that Gen. Chambers be returned to his command, having in view another raid into Middle Tennessee; which was agreed to by Gen. Taylor, who had determined upon the destruction of government stores at Johnsonville. The greater part of supplies accumulating at this point were for Sheridan's forces and those serving in Middle and East Tennessee. Gen. Chalmers reported to Gen. Forrest October 20. He ordered Buford's Division to Big Sandy, on the Tennessee river. In the meantime a small force was sent out to watch the movements of the Federals at Memphis. All the approaches to the city were barricaded with cotton, and great alarm was manifested by those in authority. On the 29th Gen. Buford captured the transport Mazeppa, heavily laden with supplies. On the 30th Gen. Chalmers captured the Undine and the transport Venus. The provisions on these boats were greatly enjoyed by the Confederates. Gen. Forrest repaired the boats and detailed crews for them, and with the land forces moved on Johnsonville. November 1, meeting the gunboats, the Undine was disabled, set fire to, and abandoned. During the rain and darkness of the night the batteries were placed in position and concealed. At twelve o'clock they opened on Johnsonville. Morton's Battery did terrible work. For an hour the conflict raged. Two gunboats were disabled, and a third one abandoned, all drifting toward the transports and heavily laden barges. At 4 p.m. every gunboat and transport was destroyed. The shells from the batteries soon finished the work. Barrels of whisky and and turpentine caught the flames, and the burning liquor ran down in torrents of liquid flame. Three gunboats, eleven transports, and eighteen barges were destroyed The Federal estimate of their loss at Johnsonville was eight million dollars.

CHAPTER XXIV.

BATTLE OF FRANKLIN, TENN.

It now becomes necessary to resume the narrative of Gen. Hood's movements after the evacuation of Atlanta. In reviewing these forces on the 18th of September President Davis had told Cheatham's Division to be of good cheer, for within a short while their faces would be turned homeward, and their feet pressing Tennessee soil.

Ten days later Gen, Hood took up his line of march toward Tennessee, with Sherman following on the 3d of October. On the 12th the Confederates took Dalton, Ga.; thence they proceeded to La Fayette, Ga.; and from that place they moved across to Gadsden, Ala., pursued by Gen. Sherman as far as Gaylesville, Ala. The latter cut himself loose from all communication with the north, and took up his celebrated movement to the sea, while Gen. Hood advanced into Tennessee, driving the enemy constantly before him, and forcing Gen. Schofield to fall back from Columbia on the 26th of November, with the loss of a large quantity of stores. "The retreat to Franklin was one of constant fighting. Skirmishing of the heaviest and deadliest character was maintained all the way. Forrest hung like a raging tiger upon the flank. . . . The Confederates pressed on— Forrest leading, Cheatham next, and Stewart following. Stephen D. Lee was still in the rear, but coming up." At Spring Hill Gen. Hood hoped to cut off

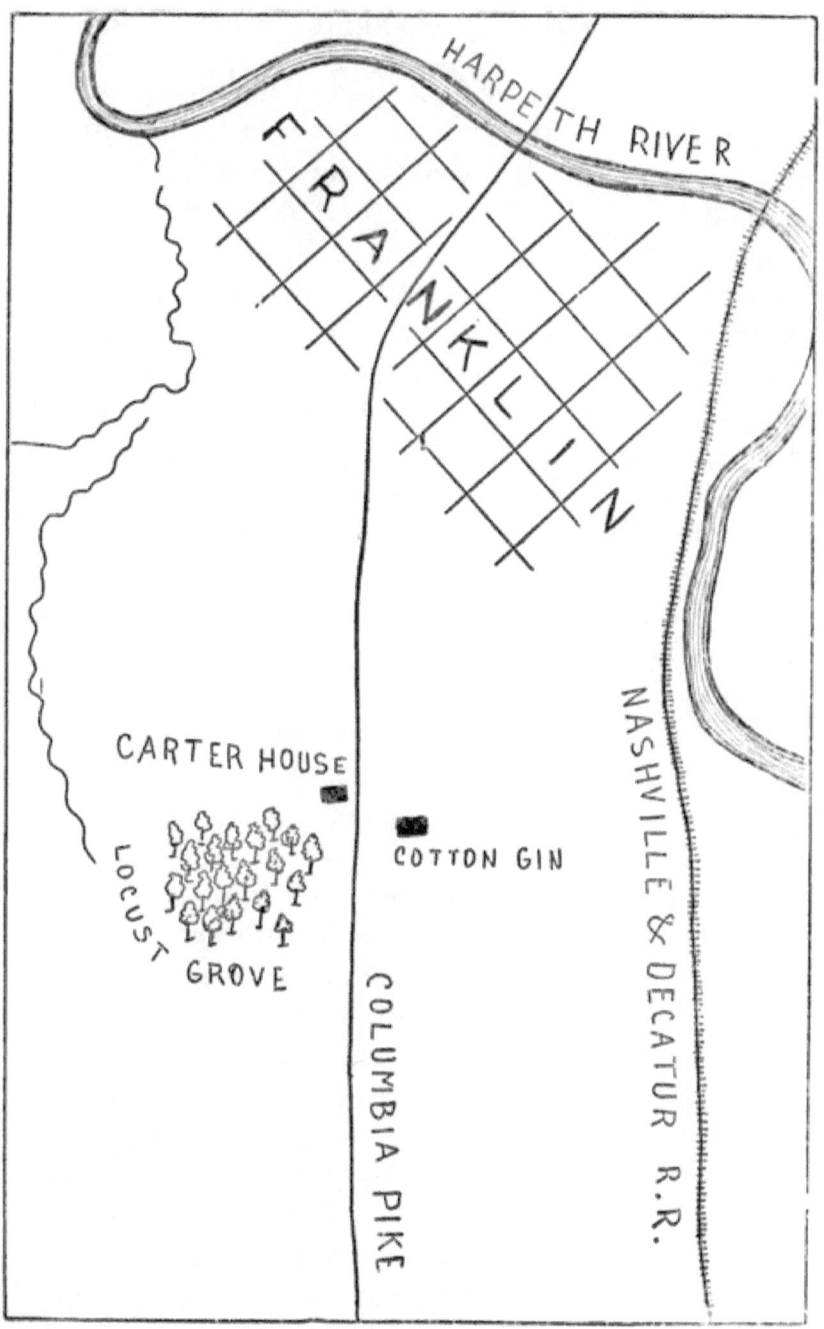

Map of Battlefield of Franklin.

the Federals' defeat, but from a misunderstanding of orders they were allowed to escape during the night. They were closely pressed the next morning, leaving evidences of their hasty retreat on every side. In this way the march was continued until the evening of November 30, when Gen. Hood found himself before the frowning breastworks of the town of Franklin. Many of the troops under him were now upon the soil of their native State, which had long been in the possession of the Federals. They could look around them and see the homes that had been denied them for many a long day, and for which now at their very thresholds they were to do battle. With such incentives as these urging them to action, at four o'clock in the afternoon they began one of the grandest attacks of the war, an attack illuminated by as sublime an exhibition of personal courage from field officer to the humblest private in the ranks as has ever blazoned the records of human bravery.

It is said the dropping of a flag by Gen. Cheatham was the signal for the charge. With a characteristic yell and tremendous force onward they advanced, stopping not nor halting, however obstinately the Federals might resist, and however thick might be the awful, bloody field of carnage with their own dead. The attack in the center by Gen. John C. Brown, of Cheatham's Corps, with Gen. Bate on his left, swept onward with a force that seemed almost irresistible. Gens. Brown, Edward Johnson, Manigault, Quarles, Cockrill, and Scales were wounded; Gen. G. W. Gordon, with part of his command, was captured inside the Federal's works. On the right Gen. Stewart's Corps fought desperately; Gen. John

Adams' brigade of Mississippians, of Loring's Division, received a fearful enfilading fire from the Federal fort on the opposite side of Harpeth River; but onward to the charge they went. In the act of leaping his charger over the Federal's works Gen. Adams was killed and fell within the intrenchments, and "Old Charley," his horse, was also killed, his form, powerful even in death, striding the Federal works, his legs reaching to the bottom of the ditch, his head on the parapet as if still breathing defiance at the foe. This was the last battle of the gallant Cleburne. Gens. Gists, Grandberry, Carter, and Strahl fell in this bloody conflict. On that crimson battleground many a knightly soul went out within sight of the firesides where the wives and little ones were praying and watching for the absent soldier's return.

A pathetic incident of this battle was the mortal wound, at the very threshold of his home, of young Carter. Here the noble deeds of gentle women beamed brightly. Col. John McGavock's residence in the battleground was used as a field hospital. With her own hands Mrs. McGavock attended to the wounded and dying with a heroism that seemed inspired. The eminent author, Rev. Henry M. Field, as a tribute to the courage of both armies, says the battle of Franklin was more desperate than that of Waterloo. Though the gray dawn of the next day saw the Federals flying toward Nashville, the victory was dearly bought. The sacrifice these soldiers offered on the altar of their country was great.

Battle of Nashville.

Through the kindness of Rev. Dr. D. C. Kelley,

of Nashville, Tenn., we are favored with his experience during the battle of Nashville. With the rank colonel, he served as a brigadier during that memorable time.

"Gen. Hood pursued the retreating Federal army to Nashville. Chalmers' Division of Cavalry that evening, in advance, reached a point from which they could see the last of Gen. Schofield's forces entering the city. No orders came from Hood to press forward. Had such orders been given, the probabilities are that the Federal army would have crossed Cumberland River without attempting to hold Nashville. Hood invested the city so far as his decreased forces would allow, after sending Forrest, with two divisions of cavalry and two brigades of infantry, toward Murfreesboro. Thomas pressed forward the work of adding fortifications to a position already strongly fortified, and waited for reënforcements until such time as he was sure his army greatly outnumbered Hood's. Hood dreamed that it was possible to rally a considerable addition to his worn, decimated, and freezing army from the country around him; he forgot that the Tennesseeans he expected to rally to him were sleeping their last sleep in Virginia and on the battlefields of the West. No young men were left to hear his bugle call. There were not enough aged men at home to care for the women and children.

"After the battle of Franklin Hood had but two ways to success open to him. One, to press into Nashville with the rear of the Federal army; the other, to retreat. He did neither, but held his ill-clad forces in the open field unprotected in the cold, until Thomas, with new recruits, chose to give battle with

Confederate army, commanded by General Hood:

Lee's Corps	4,762
Stewart's Corps	5,221
Cheatham's Corps	3,467
Artillery	1,547
Cavalry	1,700
Total of all arms	16,697

United States forces, commanded by Major-general George H. Thomas, 55,000 strong, with a reserve in Nashville.

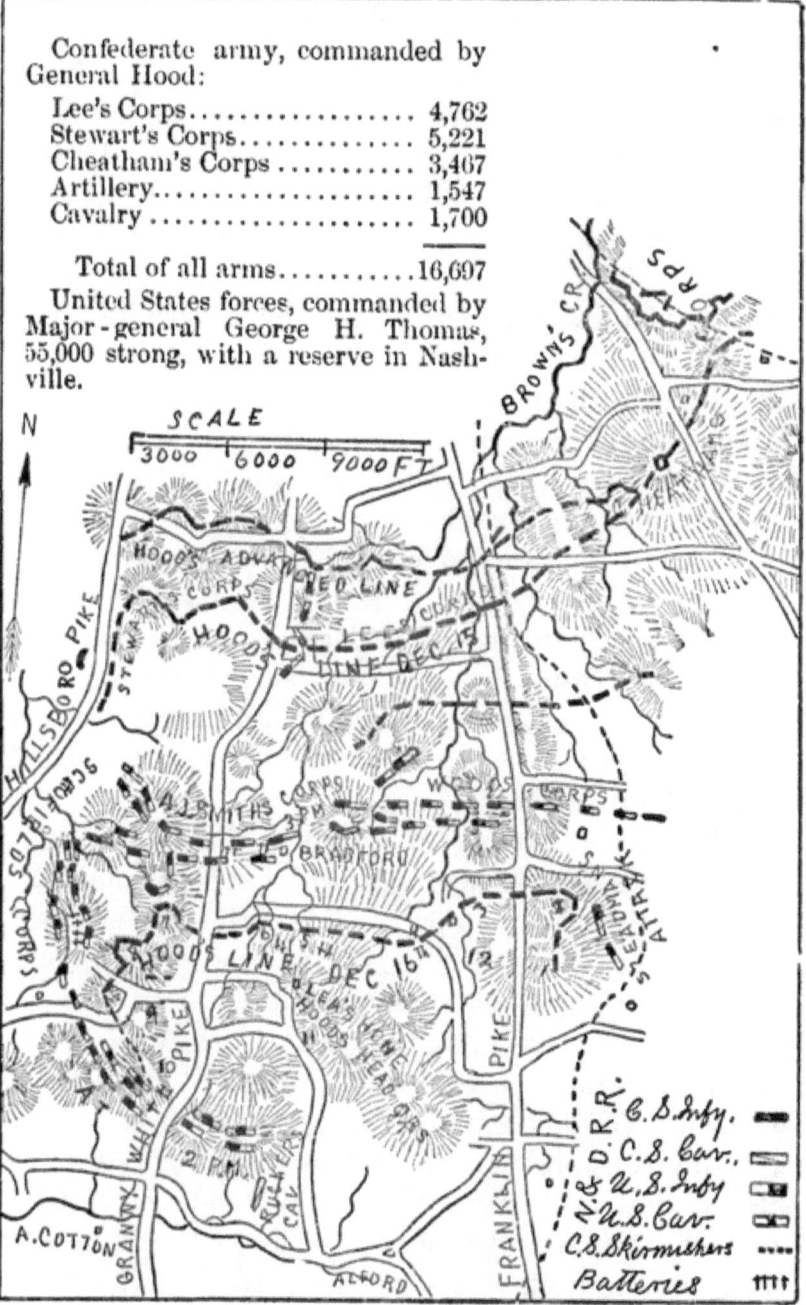

Map of the Battlefield of Nashville.

overwhelming numbers. When Thomas moved out, on December 15, the investing army extended from Brown's Creek on the right to the Cumberland river, six miles below Nashville, on the left. There was little more than a skirmish line on a good part of the ground. From the Harding pike to the river below Nashville, more than two miles, there were less than fifteen hundred cavalry. The attack was begun at this point with seven thousand Federal cavalry. The whole Confederate line repulsed the attacking forces on the first day, except the then thin line of infantry on the right of and across the Harding pike. When this part of the line gave way it left the cavalry on the left without support.

"The next morning found Hood's line shortened so that his left rested near the Hillsboro pike. The cavalry had, by a detour, marching all night, reached this pike just at daybreak with their artillery and wagon train intact.

"Hood's line, on the morning of the 16th, sought to cover the space between Brown's Creek on the right and the Hillsboro road on the left. Here, from early morning until approaching night, the battle raged. The cavalry, now less than one thousand strong, repulsed all attempts upon the part of the Federal cavalry to pass the Confederate left until late in the afternoon. The Federal forces were massed in a most advantageous position, from which their artillery enfiladed our weak line of infantry holding position near the Granny White road. Twice the Federals were driven back when charging in overwhelming numbers. Tennesseans were fighting on Tennessee soil—fighting as men fight for their own firesides. A third time the Federals moved to the charge. First, a line of skirmishers; then two dense lines came in sight, passing the summit of the hills. The veterans of many hard-fought battles knew that resistance longer was madness. Looking down their own thin line, realizing there were no reserves, they were aware that to stand longer was to invoke a stampede or surrender. Without waiting for orders, they began with firm tread to move to the rear. These men were veterans, tried and true; they did what was best. This movement compelled the retreat of the whole army. The small body of cavalry had been actively employed throughout the day resisting the effort of the Federal cavalry to pass the left flank. Soon after the retreat began.

"An order reached the commanding officer from Gen. Hood, saying: 'The army is in full retreat. Hold the Federals off my flank at all hazards.' The one brigade of Confederate cavalry had by this time been reduced to less than one thousand. Dismounting all but two squadrons, which he placed on either flank, he threw his command across the Granny White pike just in time to meet and repel the fierce charge of the Federal cavalry. For three fateful hours, until night had closed in, he held this position, rolling back onset after onset of the opposing force until he found himself about to be surrounded in the darkness. Mounting his men, by a rapid gallop he threw himself between the Federal cavalry and the rear of the army, then passing Brentwood. The Federal authorities vary as to the number of their cavalry which had been thus held in check; none of them place it less than seven thousand, some of them as high as fourteen thousand. Had this body struck Hood's flank at the hour his command was received, half his army had never crossed Harpeth River at Franklin. Two divisions of Federal cavalry are mentioned in Scribner's War Series as engaged in this night attack.

"From Brentwood to Columbia the cavalry kept in the rear of the retreating Confederates. The Federals had ten to one of fresh cavalry in pursuit, but only once did they break the stubborn line which held them at bay. At Columbia, Forrest, with Jackson's and Buford's Divisions, arrived from Murfreesboro, and, being supported by Walthall's Infantry, turned the retreat into an attack and won, out of disaster, two such victories over the pursuing forces that the Federals ceased to press the pursuit before Hood's footsore veterans reached the Tennessee river. Why the whole army was not captured by this overwhelming Federal force it is hard to understand."

Sherman's March to the Sea.

Gen. Sherman now abandons all posts south of Dalton. From Gaylorsville and Rome the work of destruction commenced. Thousands of bales of cotton, flour mills, machine shops, depots, buildings, storehouses, bridges were destroyed. The whole line back to Atlanta was one continuous track of smoke and flame. November 15 destruction began in Atlanta. Buildings covering two hundred acres had the torch applied. The heavens appeared to be one solid sheet of flame. Amid this terrible scene of suffering Gen. Sherman's bands played "John Brown's Soul Goes Marching On." The main outline of the

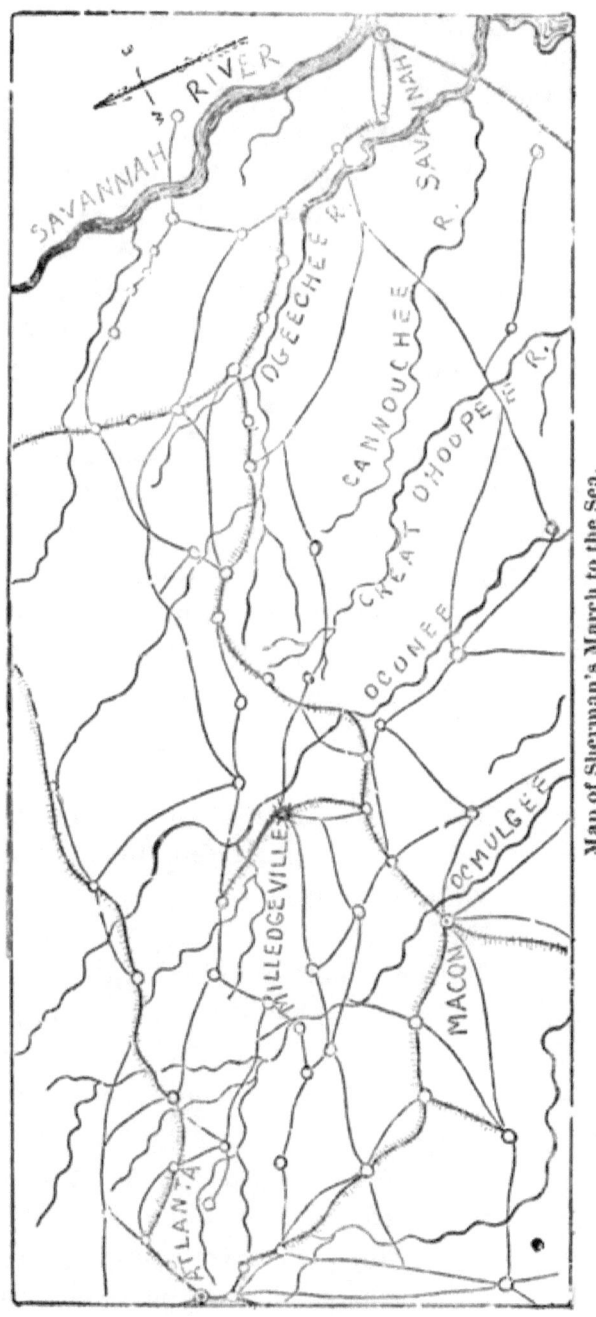

Map of Sherman's March to the Sea.

march was as follows: Gen. Howard, right on the Georgia Central road through Macon and Milledgeville to Savannah; Slocum, directly east, on the railroad from Atlanta to Augusta, burning as they went; cavalry, north of Slocum, south of Howard. Orders were given to feed man and beast on the country. Supplies in this region were abundant; transportation being difficult, Sherman's army was well fed. Slocum now moved on the Augusta roilroad. Reaching a beautiful little town called Madison, he completely demolished it. November 21 he entered Milledgeville. From that place he moved toward Augusta. He had utterly devastated the richest portion of Georgia; but now he is in the piney woods, leaving behind him four hundred miles of utter desolation and perfect wrecks of railroads, with no restraint whatever on his army.

December 2 Sherman entered a little village called Millen and destroyed it. In six columns he marched toward Savannah. Ten miles from there he encountered a small force of Hardee's Corps. December 10 he formed a line of battle and made an effort to connect with Dahlgreen's fleet, so as to capture Fort McAlister. This fort had resisted three bombardments by the Federal ironclads. A whole division was ordered for the work. Manfully they went over the parapet wall, many a one never to get out alive. The little band of Confederates fought them desperately. Knowing he was outnumbered, Gen. Hardee, while Gen. Sherman and his men were sleeping, with his army and wagon trains marched out, evacuated Savannah without the slightest molestation, and next day landed them on the Carolina shore.

This movement of Sherman's is considered a grand piece of strategy by his friends. We cannot agree to any great military merit, or anything approaching to a hero in the commander. He had no opposition; going over distance with desolation in his track was no great strategy. Yet this march is compared to Napoleon's march to Moscow.

Attempts upon Wilmington.

The next objective point of the Federals was Wilmington, N. C., especially defended by Fort Fisher. Therefore on the 22d of December we find Admiral Porter before Fort Fisher, with the largest fleet under his command the Federals had ever yet assembled. Operations were begun on the same night by the explosion of a "powder" vessel close under the walls of the fort, which was expected to destroy it. But this ingenious contrivance totally failed of its purpose, and the next day was consumed in a heavy bombardment, to which the brave garrison responded vigorously and warmly. Meantime Gen. Butler came up with a land force six thousand five hundred strong, which was to attack the fort in conjunction with the fleet. All the next day the fleet kept up a terrific cannonading, so that the earth trembled as if in the throes of an earthquake. But still the defenders of the fort worked their guns in a magnificent fashion. The land force did not risk an attack, and this expedition proved such a complete failure as to cost Gen. Butler his command.

However, the Federals were not content with their reverse from such an important point, and by January 13, 1865, they had another force, stronger by two thousand men, before the walls of Fort Fisher. During the night they had succeeded in landing and throwing up such a strong line of intrenchments that Gen. Bragg decided not to attempt to dislodge them, but to reënforce the fort. The continuous bombardment from the fleet never ceased, and, with their attention thus engaged toward defending themselves from the water, on the night of the 15th the garrison were attacked by an assaulting column four thousand strong. In spite of the fact that they were worn out and exhausted with the hard and arduous labor of manning the guns, for three long hours they resisted with a courage born of desperation, until the force of numbers compelled them to surrender, though indeed not until eight hundred of the Federals lay dead and wounded.

From this victory the Federals did not get immediate possession of the town of Wilmington, for it was not abandoned by Gen. Bragg until the latter part of February, when he retreated into the interior of the State, and left it in their hands without resistance.

Fall of Charleston and Columbia.

Almost one month from his success at Savannah Gen. Sherman again set his column in motion toward the north, with Charleston as the objective point, Gen. Hardee, perceiving that his forces were much too small to offer anything like a successful resistance, and appreciating the importance of making a juncture with Gens. Beauregard and Cheatham, after burning all government buildings and stores, abandoned to the rapacity of the Federals the historic, noble old city, which place they entered February 18.

The indentations of shells, the marks of fire, the ruins on every side, stood like grand though somber and sorrowful monuments to the heroism of a people who had endured so bravely and so patiently all the horrors and misfortunes that come in the train of war—siege and bombardment, rapine and murder—yet so noble and eloquent in her ruins, so very typical of the whole South, whose very scars were a glory and honor to her, telling a grand story of how she had fought and toiled and struggled and labored in the face of adverse circumstances.

Leaving Branchville, Gen. Sherman still continued his devastating march. Columbia met even a more terrible fate than Charleston. A large portion of the town was given to the devouring flames, while *no part* of it escaped the thirst for robbery and plunder which had taken complete possession of the Federal army. Citizens were rendered houseless and homeless, and whatever valuables they had the Federals appropriated to their own use.

On this band of invaders advanced; nor did they abate those tactics that had first characterized their entrance into the State of Georgia. On the 6th of March they crossed the Great Pedee river, against the towns of Laurel Hill and Montpelier, N. C., meeting with no resistance until March 10, when Gen. Kilpatrick's forces received a severe blow at the hands of Gen. Wade Hampton. On the 16th the Federals came up with Gen. Hardee, who was fortified between Cape Fear River and Black Creek. The latter gallantly sustained three assaults from two corps under Gen. Slocum, and then retreated. The severity of the engagement is shown by the fact that the Federals lost thirty-three hundred men, while the Confederates lost only four hundred and fifty.

BATTLE OF BENTONVILLE.

On the 19th of February Gen. Bragg and Stewart's Corps reached an elevation twelve miles from Bentonville and sixteen miles from a place called Smithfield. Gen. Hardee arrived on the scene of action; Hope's Division which had been across the road; Stewart's Corps on the right. The attack was vigorous. Gens. McLaw and Taliaferro were placed on Gen. Stewart's right. The Federals were severely repulsed on the left by Gen. Loring's Division; on the right the Confederates drove the Fourteceth Corps a mile to a dense thicket.

This battle began at three o'clock and continued until dark. Had Gen. Wheeler's cavalry not been kept by a swollen stream, the Federal rear would have had a panic. After burying the dead and removing the wounded of both armies, General Johnston resumed his first position. Gen. Johnston's object in making this fight was to cripple Gen. Sherman before he could form a junction with Schofield, but as it was the Confederates gained a victory. With fourteen thousand soldiers they met the Fourteenth and Twentieth Corps of the Federals, also Kilpatrick's Cavalry, an aggregate of forty thousand men. On the 20th Sherman's whole army was in front of Gen. Johnston, the Confederates being compelled to fight to bring off the wounded. Before daybreak on the 22d Gen. Johnston moved toward Smithfield, his loss in three days being fourteen hundred and ninety-nine wounded and eight hundred prisoners.

Sherman effected the junction with Schofield—an army of one hundred thousand men. Sherman now hastened to City Point for a conference with President Lincoln and Gen. Grant.

Capture of Mobile.

Mobile was well protected, supplies for a siege abundant, Gen. Maury in command. Eight thousand soldiers were the whole force. On the 26th of March Gen. Canby, with sixty thousand troops, appeared, accompanied by a heavy fleet of gunboats, in front of Fort Blakely and Spanish Fort, which were a distance of twelve miles from Mobile. Gen. Randall Gibson, of Louisiana, conducted the defense of Spanish Fort with the Louisiana veteran brigade, an Alabama brigade, the Twenty-Second Louisiana Heavy Artillery, and three companies of light artillery. The Federals, with overwhelming numbers, were bold and defiant. On the 8th of April Gen. Maury gave orders for the removal of all the forces from the forts to the city. Gen. St. John Liddell, of Louisiana, had charge of Fort Blakely. The garrison consisted of Mississippians and Missourians. Col. Spence's cavalry force was ordered to burn the cotton. After a noble defense during the four years, beautiful Mobile surrendered at last. During the entire struggle her ports were used as the best entry for blockade runners, bringing medicines and other necessaries for the army as well as the people. In this beautiful city, interred in Soldiers' Rest (Confederate Cemetery), lie the remains of Gen. Braxton Bragg, also by his side soldiers from all parts of our Southland, each having a marble head and foot stone bearing their name. In the Catholic burial ground repose the bodies of Admiral Semmes and our poet priest, Father Ryan, a simple slab with the beautiful inscription, *In Memoriam*, marking their resting place.

CHAPTER XXV.

THE END.

ONE needs no prophetic eye to see that the final act in the great drama is near at hand—that the catastrophe is approaching. The North, with her mighty hosts, is tightening and drawing in her lines. The South, though she had gained victory after victory, never had a force adequate to consummate the war in a complete victory for the Confederacy. Therefore, from the beginning it was merely a question of time when those very first victories themselves, as paradoxical as it may seem, hastened defeat; for they cost many lives, and the Confederate dead that lay upon the battlefields of Murfreesboro, Shiloh, Gettysburg, Chancellorsville, and other places, could not be replaced with the living; whereas the North was rich in men and resources, and her armies stretched in an almost unbroken line from the Potomac to the Rio Grande. What could a Confederate victory avail against such a power, with the whole world for a recruiting ground? The South had worn herself literally out with the victories won from the Federals, and now, with a depleted army and an exhausted commissary, one only wonders in admiration that divine courage could so triumph over the weakness of human physical nature as to enable those veterans of the Army of Virginia and of the Army of Tennessee to resist so long and so bravely.

Peace Conference.

Early in the year 1865 a conference took place between President Lincoln, Mr. Seward, and three commissioners appointed by President Davis: Messrs. Stephens, Campbell, and Hunter. The meeting was held on board a steamer anchored in Hampton Roads; but the government at Washington still insisted upon terms which the Confederacy would not accept, and nothing tangible resulted from the conference.

Consequently hostilities in Northern Virginia were again resumed by Sheridan once more raiding up the Shenandoah valley. Near Waynesboro, toward the end of February, he fell upon the weakened remnants of Gen. Early's Division, defeated them, and took as many as thirteen hundred prisoners. Thence the Federals proceeded on their course of destruction, and finally joined Gen. Meade near Petersburg.

Closing Conflicts.

The Federals continued to batter with their huge forces the weakened, poorly fed, and ill-clothed lines in the immediate vicinity of Richmond. On the 6th of February they flung themselves against Pegram's Division, and were on the point of overpowering it when Gen. Evans arrived with Gen. Gordon's Division. Charge after charge was made, but still the Federals managed to maintain themselves until the Confederates were further reënforced by Gen. Mahone. With their former enthusiasm and spirit they swept the Federals before them in confusion to the shelter of their fortifications at Hatcher's Run.

This was followed by a well-planned attack upon the Federals' position at Hare's Hill, near Appomattox. Here again was a glimmer of the glory of the former days of the war. Early on the morning of March 25 Gen. Gordon surprised and captured a considerable portion of the Federal works, repulsing brilliantly two successive attacks of their infantry to regain them. But the Confederates were forced by the artillery which the Federals massed against them to abandon the position which they had taken, carrying back with them, however, seventeen pieces of artillery and six hundred prisoners.

This partial, spasmodic success was more than counterbalanced on the 1st and 2d of April by the blows which the Federals struck against the gray wall around Petersburg, now grown so thin that it would seem sheer madness for them to attempt to offer resistance to the heavy, unbroken columns of the Federals. However, they fought in the face of despair itself, and were pierced by the numerous hosts of the Federals.

Here in the closing scenes Gen. A. P. Hill, another of the South's great leaders, laid down his life for the Confederate cause, and was placed in the muster roll of immortals as one of the heroes in the struggle. But yet a greater loss was in store for the South. The clouds were gathering to cast their shadows over the brightness of that spring day. The city of their love, for the defense of which their best, their truest blood had been poured out—in front of whose fortifications lay the bones of those whose return was watched for in the Carolinas, in Tennessee, in Georgia, in Louisiana, in Mississippi, in Alabama, and in far-off Texas—was soon to be given over into the hands of the foeman.

While President Davis was attending church on the 2d of April a notice was brought to him from Gen. Lee, telling him of the disaster at Petersburg, which made the evacuation of Richmond necessary on that very night. As President Davis retired the services were put to an end, and the dread news soon spread all over the city, causing many a cheek to blanch and many a strong heart to throb in unspeakable sorrow over the loss of this the last stronghold and the only hope of the young government that had lived its life in the midst of the troublous times of war. Night came, and Richmond was without defenders; and, to add to the gloom of the situation many large warehouses had been burned by the retreating Confederates, that their contents might not fall into the hands of the victor. In this conflagation it would seem that the hopes which in the moments of victory promised a glorious consummation in the formation of a free, happy, contented union of individual States, into which jealousy, passion, and prejudice could find no place, were being consumed and only the dead ashes of despair were left them.

Early on the morning following the evacuation a detachment of cavalry from Gen. Weitzel's Division planted the United States flag upon the dome of the capitol, and later in the day Gen. Weitzel himself entered the city and put it under martial law.

The Surrender.

The fortunes of the little band under Gen. Lee need not be pressed much farther. They were now on the north side of the Appomattox river, with the Federals pressing and harassing them on all sides, and gradually capturing squad after squad of his worn and exhausted troops. Against such a force as that of the Federals it would be utterly useless for him to hurl his decimated columns. Moreover, many of his men, foreseeing the inevitable result, had left the ranks, and were seeking to escape to their homes in order to avoid subjecting themselves to the humiliation of a surrender. The Federal commander himself clearly perceived the sure doom that awaited the once glorious army of Northern Virginia—still grand even in the midst of its misfortunes—and on the 7th of April sent a demand for the surrender of the troops that had made themselves the admiration of the world. After a correspondence lasting through two days, the following terms were proposed by Gen. Grant, and agreed to by Gen. Lee on the 9th:

> Roll of all officers and men to be made in duplicate, and one copy to be given to an officer to be designated by me and the other to be retained by such officers as you may designate; the officers to give their individual parole not to take up arms against the government of the United States until properly exchanged, and each company or regimental commander to sign a like parole for the men of their commands. The arms, artillery, and public property to be packed and stacked and turned over by me to officers appointed to receive them. This will not embrace the side arms of the officers nor their private horses or baggage.
>
> This done, each officer and man will be allowed to return to their homes, not to be disturbed by United States authority so long as they observe their parole and the laws in force where they may reside.

The conference between Gen. Lee and Gen. Grant was held in the residence of Mr. Wilmer McLean, at Appomattox C. H. The meeting was of the simplest

Col. John Overton's Residence, Gen. Hood's Headquarters at the Battle of Nashville. (See page 168.)

Mr. Wilmer McLean's Residence, Where Gen. Lee Surrendered.

character. Each conducted himself with dignity and courtesy, the Federal commander displaying a magnanimity worthy of recording in that he subjected Gen. Lee to no humiliating forms and conditions. The result was that Gen. Lee issued the following order to his troops:

General Order No. 9.

After four years of arduous service, marked by unsurpassed courage and fortitude, the Army of Northern Virginia has been compelled to yield to overwhelming numbers and resources.

I need not tell the brave survivors of so many hard-fought battles who have remained steadfast to the last that I have consented to this result from no distrust of them; but, feeling that valor and devotion could accomplish nothing that would compensate for the loss that must have attended the continuation of the contest, I determined to avoid the sacrifice of those whose past services have endeared them to their countrymen.

By the terms of agreement, officers and men can return to their homes and remain until exchanged. You will take with you the satisfaction that proceeds from the consciousness of duty faithfully performed, and I earnestly pray that a merciful God will extend to you his blessings and protection.

With an unceasing admiration of your constancy and devotion to your country, and a grateful remembrance of your kind and generous consideration of myself, I bid you an affectionate farewell. R. E. LEE, *General*.

April 10, 1865.

With this ends the story of the Army of Northern Virginia. A glorious story it is, too. They had fought a good fight, and had kept the faith with the country and the principles which they had espoused. They did their duty nobly, and have left to the keeping of the land for which they battled the record of their sublime devotion and incomparable courage. Taking leave of their leader, in whom they ever had a steadfast faith, whether in victory or defeat, they turned their weary steps to their desolated homes, where fond hearts were waiting to welcome the battle-scarred soldier; and with the same grand courage with which they had brightened the pages of human history, they went to work to rehabilitate the wasted farm and the deserted workshop.

The surrender of the other divisions of the Confederates necessarily followed that of Gen. Lee in rapid succession. April 18 Gen. Joseph E. Johnston surrendered near Greensboro, N. C.; Gen. Dick Taylor to Gen. Canby at Citronelle, Ala., May 4; and Gen. Kirby Smith to the same general at Baton Rouge, La., on the 26th. Thus ended the long and arduous struggle which the South made for the rights she had under the Constitution, and in this struggle those who wore the gray and stepped to the inspiring strains of "Dixie" under the banner of the Southern cross, decked with its stars, have made their uniform a symbol of the sublimest courage of the soldier and the truest devotion of the patriot.

APPENDIX.

We are indebted to Gen. Marcus J. Wright for the following:

WASHINGTON, D. C., January 12, 1899.

The official report of the adjutant general of the United States army, October 9. 1880, reports the number of men furnished the United States army during the civil war as 2,778,-304. Aggregate reduced to three years' standard, 2,320,369. Absence of many of the Confederate muster rolls makes it impossible to give the exact number in the Confederate army, but the best estimates put the whole number during the war at between six and seven hundred thousand, not exceeding the latter number.

The losses in the Federal army, from reports of the adjutant general to the surgeon general, were: Killed in battle, 44,238; died of wounds, 49,204; suicide, homicide, and executions, 526; died of disease, 186,216; unknown causes, 24,184. Total, 304,639. Of these, 269,265 were white and 33,380 colored.

Dr. Joseph Jones, surgeon Confederate army, gives estimate of Confederate losses, of which I send you a rough memorandum.

Very truly,   MARCUS J. WRIGHT.

General Wright also furnishes the following statistics compiled by the late Dr. Joseph Jones, surgeon general of the Confederate army:

Year.	Killed.	Wounded.	Prisoners.
1861	1,315	4,054	2,772
1862	18,522	6,859	48,300
1863	11,876	55,313	71,211
1864-65	22,000	70,000	80,000
Total	53,713	136,226	202,283

If deaths from disease be added, the sum total will represent the entire loss. The returns of the field and general hospitals are known for 1861-62:

Confederates killed in battle, 1861-62	19,597
Deaths caused by wounds, field hospitals	1,623
Deaths caused by wounds, general hospitals	2,618
Deaths caused by disease, field hospitals	14,597
Deaths caused by disease, general hospitals	16,741
Total 1861-62	55,176
Total wounded in C. S. A., 1861-62	72,713
Total prisoners in C. S. A., 1861-62	51,072
Total discharged in C. S. A., 1861-62	16,940
Total wounded and discharged prisoners, 1861-62	140,725

If it be fair to assume that the total mortality of 1863-64 was fully equal to that of 1862, then the total deaths in the Confederate Army, 1861-65, were at least 160,000, exclusive of deaths in the northern prisons, which would swell the number to near 185,000; and if the deaths from the discharged for wounds and disease and amongst the sick and wounded on furloughs be added, the grad total will not fall far short of 200,000. According to this calculation, the deaths from disease were about three times as numerous as those resulting from the casualties in battle.

There is but one conclusion for the dispassionate historian to admit, and that is: the downfall of the Confederacy was due to the overpowering numbers of the Federals. The only just basis of comparison between military forces of the North and the South is to be found in a careful statement of the population. If we add to the free States those that followed their lead (Delaware, Maryland, Missouri, and Kentucky) and to these the districts under command of the Federals from an early period of the war, (say half of Tennessee and a third of Virginia), we have a population, by the census of 1860, of 23,485,722 on the Federal side. This leaves the Confederacy 7,662,325. Called by President Lincoln from April 15, 1861, to April, 1865, 2,859,000 soldiers; from the South, 600,000.

www.ingramcontent.com/pod-product-compliance
Lightning Source LLC
Chambersburg PA
CBHW030818190426
43197CB00036B/593